If You Are
What You Eat,
Your Company Is What It

Thinks

By **J.A. Schmid**

Copyright © 2014 by J.A. Schmid

All rights reserved

Cover Photography and Design by Angel Ruff

Editing by J.M. Morris

No part of this book may be reproduced in any form or by any electronic or mechanical means including information storage and retrieval systems, without permission in writing from the author. The only exception is by a reviewer, who may quote short excerpts in a review.

This book is a work of fiction. Names, characters, places, and incidents either are products of the author's imagination or are used fictitiously. Any resemblance to actual persons, living or dead, events, or locales is entirely coincidental.

J.A. Schmid

www.oakleafconsulting.com

Published in the United States of America

First Published: September 2014

Dedication

To Jackie

For her faith, support, and teamwork on our life's journey raising four wonderful children.

Why I wrote this Book

Stepping out of the daily fray is difficult at best. We're so attuned to the rituals, customs, habits, and traditions we can no longer see them for what they are, how they envelop and define us. I wrote this book to help the reader pull up and see with a fresh set of eyes.

Corporate Think is the product of leadership watching. Observable actions are a leader's teaching tool – their *voice* – not the missives, presentations, proclamations, or what is incorporated in handbooks or on company web pages. *Corporate Think* controls what gets done, how it gets done, and the rules of getting it done. It establishes what is okay and what is not. It is the framework for the code of conduct and ethical standards. It is the moderator of a company's brand.

Corporate stories and legends, the retelling of leadership actions, are the fabric of *Corporate Think*. These stories and legends are the models for engagement with customers, colleagues, ownership, and the governments and the communities in which they maintain a footprint. They are the organization's *mental muscle memory*. The *thinking processes* of a company are its *most strategic building blocks*. They define what it is. The collapse or success of companies is rooted in these processes.

This book is a collection of short stories telling the tales of a variety of *corporate thinking scenarios* with their resulting rituals and outcomes. Each chapter is written to be a *catalyst for self-observing*. Seeing your environment clearly and accepting its reality is the first step of a journey you can choose to take, or not.

TABLE OF CONTENTS

CHAPTER 1 **"GO ALONG TO GET ALONG"**	1
CHAPTER 2 **"PARANOIA"**	9
CHAPTER 3 **"HARDWIRED"**	19
CHAPTER 4 **"THE DREADED CUSTOMER"**	27
CHAPTER 5 **"YES WE CAN"**	35
CHAPTER 6 **"BUT . . ."**	43
CHAPTER 7 **"MAVERICKS"**	51
CHAPTER 8 **"RUMORS"**	59
CHAPTER 9 **"SOUNDERS"**	65
CHAPTER 10 **"FLOCK BIRDS"**	73
CHAPTER 11 **"BE GOOD OR BE GOOD AT IT"**	79
CHAPTER 12 **"PINNIPEDS"**	85
CHAPTER 13 **"TOTEMS"**	93
CHAPTER 14 **"IT APPEARS MY HYPOCRISY KNOWS NO BOUNDS"**	97
CHAPTER 15 **"THE _____ CLUB"**	103
EPILOGUE	107

If You Are What You Eat, Your Company Is What It Thinks

Chapter 1

"GO ALONG TO GET ALONG"

There is just something wrong about a "normal distribution", the bell shaped curve. When you think about people, what the heck is normal? You are told to be different, to set yourself apart. But when you get too far one way or another outside the 1-Sigma band of behavioral normality, you're in trouble.

Now Ed wasn't always as physically big as he is now. He'd been a late bloomer as his mom used to say. He was seventeen and almost through high school before his hormones kicked in. College was awkward. Dealing with an additional six inches of height his freshman year was difficult. He had to relearn everything. It was like switching from driving a short front end car to a long front end one. He kind of misjudged everything and ended up running into a lot of things. Eye-hand coordination wasn't the greatest back then. Ed couldn't pass a DUI test sober for the longest while.

But all things change. Ed hit 6' 5" and 195 pounds. But in most ways he still thought of himself as inconspicuous. He matured into a big guy with a short guy state of mind. Growing up hadn't been all that easy – but who can't claim that. Ed had learned to cope in different ways, but the one that seemed to work the best was to be part of the crowd. There was safety in the anonymity of numbers.

If You Are What You Eat, Your Company Is What It Thinks

Maybe it's a herd instinct as some claim - banding together. After all, a posse must be right – said so in the TV westerns Ed had watched growing up.

Being a non-athletic small guy in high school had affected Ed. He'd studied more than most. With minimal after school activities, he tended to come right home and do his homework. Some never figure out that going to class and doing the homework guarantees a B. Ed did – albeit under his parents' continuous scrutiny. So Ed finished high school, with great grades in science and math (you just can't BS an answer in those subjects). When he went to college, he stayed the course and graduated with an Electrical Engineering degree. He had kept up the habit of class and homework, so finding a job with his superior grades was a piece of cake.

Ed landed with a great global company. First thing Ed was immersed in was the "on-boarding" process for new hires. It was a "birds of a feather and pigs and swine" thing happening. He and his peers were getting pigeonholed through the process – sales types belong here, manufacturing belong there, researchers here, and on and on.

During their first year, new hires went through a three-month progressive rotation. No one stayed long enough in any one place do anything of merit – but regardless everyone was given a 360-degree evaluation at the end of each rotation as they shipped out of one department to the next. When the yearlong rotation cycle was complete, the birds of a feather were all together, as well as the pigs and the swine. But the rats and mice (the organizational outliers) had a choice. And that choice was a two-month severance pay plus outplacement assistance or nothing.

If You Are What You Eat, Your Company Is What It Thinks

Nobody had stayed anywhere long enough to do anything close to good – or bad either. The "rodents" were told they just weren't a fit – and the hiring mistake had been a mutual one (whatever a mutual mistake is). Ed was shocked. The "rodents" were the cool group. They were the ones who organized the parties and got weekend activities together. They were also the ones who spoke up in meetings and asked what was on the mind of every newbie (but were afraid to ask). They were the ones who pitched their ideas in meetings, even though the newbies were so new it was hard to make a sane argument out of what they said.

Ed had no problems. Everyone liked him. He got along with everyone. He was a big guy, but he didn't have an attitude. Ed reflected that all the "rodents" had a "big guy" attitude regardless of physical stature. Ed learned the golden rule of advancing – "Go along to get along". To that end, Ed learned and mastered several principles. The first was "In a meeting, always jockey to be the last one to speak." Ed had watched the scramble of his want-a-be peers all clambering to catch the spotlight. Everyone wanted to impart their wisdom and be noticed. It was like watching king-of-the-hill, and Ed had watched a lot of that growing up. What he quickly learned was the last person to speak was the most likely to be remembered.

The second principle Ed learned was "Never give an answer – always ask a question". There are two kinds of questions. The first show concern – "Are you okay?" The second kinds of questions are those that end with an implied "stupid." Like "What did you think was going to happen?" Asking these second kinds was the step ladder to getting ahead.

When Ed got those two principles in gear, his management career started to move. Some of his upwardly mobile peers tried an alternate principle, "Never be for anything." This principle is hard to play out. Its highest form is being negative about everything. When you are negative about something, there is no risk. If whatever it is you were against doesn't work out – "I told you so." If it does you can say nothing and hope no one remembers, or remind everyone that you weren't aware of certain key facts, and preach the importance of sharing all the facts before asking for an opinion. Risk is only incurred when you are for something – you can be wrong. So Ed learned never to be for anything (or jump on late when whatever was on the table was a sure done deal). His career flight path was looking great for entry into middle management. He honed his skills of keeping his mouth shut until everyone else spoke, and when he spoke it was always a question.

Ed's popularity continued to grow – everybody likes to be around a big guy, particularly when they don't act like one. As Ed rose, "going along to get along" got a lot harder. All his peers had also learned to speak last, and the "only ask a question principle". The controversial types were left in the dust or mostly gone. Creating a controversy was out of the question if you didn't want to stunt your career growth.

Something had to give. The 1-Sigma band of normality was getting tighter and tighter as the high potential group population got smaller and more competitive. Ed was beginning to panic. It was like a bicycle road race. The peloton of future senior management prospects was disciplined. If they didn't stay together and act as a single unit, no one would win. But, on the other hand, if you didn't break out, how did you win? Everyone also knew there was another peloton composed of those that had replaced them in their old assignments coming up from behind. Staying together was critical to safety but then it was dangerous too. It was a true conundrum. You couldn't talk to your peers about it. And talking to your reports was organizational suicide.

Ed woke bolt upright one night. He felt like a tree had just fallen on the house (Ed had been worrying about that too). But that wasn't it. It was one word coursing through his head that had awakened him – MENTOR. That was the ticket he thought – "I need my personal Yoda. But where can I find one, and how?" There would be no more sleep for Ed that night. Asking for a mentor could be a sign of weakness.

Mentor is a strange word. It doesn't seem to have anything to do with the character in Greek mythology from whence it came. Or did it have more to do with a character in a French book that came out years later? Regardless, the mentor and mentee terms came to be. Some professions continue the practice formally. In medicine, it is common for a young doctor to be paired with an older doc. Ed had found his solution to breaking from the management peloton.

"But how to do it" Ed pondered. There had been talk about mentoring. There had even been some trials, albeit they went badly. Seems the idea that the trial mentors had in their heads was to point out to their mentees that they weren't just like them. But when a male mentor told their female mentee that they aren't "going anywhere in this company until they grow a set of balls," well that ended the mentor program trial. So this was going to be a tough obstacle for Ed to get over. At which point the alarm went off, and Ed crawled out of bed.

In the shower, Ed laid out his plan. Now why do you suppose in the shower is where some of the most productive thinking of the day occurs? Maybe you just feel free, and it affects your brain. Maybe naked is a free thinking state. It could explain why toddlers run around the house naked with parents in pursuit after pulling a dirty diaper off them. There could be a business analogy here. Maybe thinking of your business as a butt naked toddler would create a mental innovative leap? Ed wondered what the diaper would be in this business analogy. And who is the pooh-pooh in the metaphor?

Later that day Ed caught up with the VP to whom he reported, and laid out the idea of getting back into mentoring and wanting to be the beta project for the restart. Ed had broken the golden rule of "not being for anything." The VP quietly took him by the elbow into an empty office, closed the door, and said, "I thought you were smarter than this Ed!" From that point on in the conversation, all Ed heard was "Blah Blah lawsuit blah blah blah albatross blah blah blah head up your blah blah blah." Ed knew a career ender. It came with keywords and phrases. No specific pattern. You just knew it when you heard it.

He rethought every step of his career. He'd been so careful. He finally concluded he'd panicked and gotten impatient. He should have just held his position in the peloton. Then it came to Ed, the final rule – "Wait for your peers to falter, and then run them over". And that's pretty much what happened in the ensuing months. Word got out that Ed was weak and needed a mentor. Ed was like a chicken that had gotten nicked up. It only takes the sniff of blood to get the whole henhouse coming after you. As with chickens there was no coup de grace, just continuous little pecks until graciously someone removes you to safety as the blood begins to flow freely.

After a suitable period of "this too could happen to you" display, Ed's boss removed him to safety. But life was good. Ed had landed on a comfortable plateau. There he would stay, watching the game of "going along to get along", and enjoying the ride.

Consensus often cuts short bold undeveloped ideas. It too often subverts the expression of new ideas and pushes thinking to the centrist commonly held view. Step changes are the province of outliers that when pursued develop into innovations.

Ask yourself this. When an outlying thought is expressed are people's first reactions to prove it's wrong and that it won't work? Or do people jump in to help and try to make it work until it either floats or it sinks of its own weight?

Is an objection or dissent viewed as obstruction? Is an intuitive leap branded as weird? The much sought after consensus if not well managed can become a short circuit robbing an organization of what could be, and miring it in what is. "Going along to get along," often mistaken as consensus, is a poison pill. It is an insidious form of "corporate think".

If You Are What You Eat, Your Company Is What It Thinks

Chapter 2

"PARANOIA"

When had staff meetings become a court martial? Fred couldn't remember. It wasn't any specific date or time. It just seemed to have happened. Maybe it was when Cliff, the founder and CEO, got reading glasses. Looking at you over the top of them tended to weird you out. Maybe we all just developed a Pavlovian defensive response that continued to escalate when he'd give you "the look".

Cliff didn't particularly like standup presentations. The inescapable adrenaline rush left him trembling. Maybe that set the stage. Regardless, staff meetings were now a nightmare. It didn't matter who started it or how or why – they just were. Everyone came in suspecting everyone else of ill intentions.

Back at the beginning, we all worked to help each other out when tough issues hit. We'd jump in to figure out a fix together. Now we all seemed to hop on when somebody was in trouble – trying to push each other's heads under the troubled waters of the moment. We did it without thinking. It was pathetic.

With resignation, Fred picked up his files and went off to play the staff meeting "gotcha game." That Friday's staff meeting played out as usual; each staff member giving their review with Charlie, the CFO, throwing out fruitless factoids of frustration and asking fall-on-your sword kinds of questions. Charlie was always a bit that way, but he seemed to have mastered it when we weren't looking.

"Why is overtime up 0.002536% over the same month last year at the Laredo Plant." A voice was screaming in Fred's head "Who cares! Like this is the stuff we are supposed to be talking about."

Fred waited for his turn on the rotisserie knowing full well he would be skewered, and he would be scribbling follow-up notes for his organization just like everyone else in the room. When the meeting was over everyone scurried back to their offices. "We used to go out for lunch together or order in something. What the heck had happened to us?" Fred thought.

As he wrote follow-up emails to his organization, he imagined a gigantic toilet flushing as all the senior staff did the same and checked "High Importance" before clicking send. Within minutes, the whole organization would be covered in pooh. Email created that ability. No matter where you were in the world, you could dole out insanity at near the speed of light to an unbounded cc. list. And then everyone "responding to all" to defend themselves against any direct or implied accusations. It was like setting off an endless "human wave" at a sports stadium.

He wondered what people were saying "out there". Was there an electronic signal sent out to sound the emergency horns at the plants, or was there an automated notification system causing every cell phone in sales to begin sounding Chopin's "Funeral March", or something to signal that the executive suite had just flushed a number two and it was now time to pick through it? Chow time!

Fred hated that he had become a part of this. He had tried to get Cliff's attention – but Cliff didn't see it as a problem. "People need pressure to perform well" was Cliff's mantra. In the beginning, staff didn't need to create the pressure – it was all-pervading. We had a 24/7 street fight on our hands getting the business off the ground.

Fred thought back on it. When the business started, there was nothing to lose. They were much younger then. Cliff had fronted all the capital and had been generous giving out sweat equity. Back then none of us had a whole lot of personal responsibility to worry about – just ourselves. We were all indestructible. Nothing could beat us. The business had grown along with our lifestyles. From just a handful of us, we'd expanded steadily. There were now over 1,700 people who depended on us being right.

With that weighing on his mind, he left the office to get to his car. On his way out, he passed the shredder room. Even with the soundproofing it was still loud. Charlie, the CFO, was in there with his staff. Everyone suspected something unseemly went on in the shredder room when the accounting group assembled there. Fred stopped at the window and peered inside. Charlie smiled and waved. The others turned and gave Fred stone-faced zombie looks, and continued to feed the insatiable appetite of the mechanical memory eraser.

Fred drove off to a fast-food drive-through and went to the nearby park to sit and enjoy lunch. When he had finished, Fred didn't feel like going back to the office. It was too pretty a day to be cooped up inside. He decided to call Jim. Jim was the Plant Manager of the Casanova Creek Plant Site. Fred and he had developed a close camaraderie while they worked to make it rise from an empty field.

Jim always picked up his cell phone when Fred called.

"Hey Fred!"

"Jimbo! Got any good email lately?"

"Why are you asking?" Jim said in an entirely different tone. "This isn't a pop quiz is it?"

Fred knew he'd stuck his foot in it.

"Well, I'm just sort of missing the old days, and thought I'd call," he said.

Ol' Jim still wasn't talking. "Darn," Fred thought, "I'm in a tight spot."

"How long have we known each other Jim?"

"Am I on the speaker phone?" Jim replied.

"Nope, I'm on a bench in the park. Only me, the squirrels, birds and the trees," Fred said trying to remain upbeat and casual.

"Are you recording this?"

This conversation was going nowhere.

"No Jim."

Silence

"Okay Jim. I was looking for a friend, somebody who remembered when we cared."

Still silence.

"Jim, I'm sorry I bothered you. Say hello to Janice and the kids."

"Hold on," Jim replied. "Look, you and I aren't who we were. Maybe we haven't changed, but the company has, and I just don't feel comfortable talking."

"We used to talk about everything," Fred said with honest remorse. "I miss that."

"I do too."

"Well, what are we going to do about it?"

"I'll call your hand. Lay down your cards, and I'll listen."

Now Fred felt a twinge of uncertainty. "Are you recording this?"

Jim laughed, "Nope."

"OK – I'll start. What do you guys in the field call this barrage of email that gets started every Friday after our staff meeting?"

"A shitstorm."

"Fair enough. We're talking the same language. I hate it too." Fred said.

After a pause Jim replied "Me too. But what am I supposed to do about it? It's Cliff's company. What are you doing about it? You say you hate it – fix it. You've got everyone second guessing everyone else. You've got the CFO talking about taking risks. What does he know? His idea of risk is totally one sided – just numbers in a spreadsheet. Starting this company was a risk. Everyone who came on board kept their resume ready. There was no such thing as retirement savings. We were all saving to weather the storm if the business went south and we were out on the street. We were in it together, maybe not to the same degree, but you couldn't tell that by watching any of us."

"And what's with Cliff? Has he lost his mind? Who is writing that stuff he is sending out? Is this endgame? Are we supposed to be playing not to lose? The people in accounting are like a case of chiggers. I feel like I've got a fly on every wall in this place reporting back instantly to the mothership."

Fred continued listening.

"The accounting department has turned into a tumor. They've got everyone covering their butts. The guy assigned here has become useless. With the new enterprise software system, he can't even tell me what things cost because the new accounting module isn't meant to do that. I write bad performance reviews on the system, and I hear it from the CFO. Our accounting guy thinks he's bulletproof. This 'Plant Controller' title has gone to his head. He goes around asking more and more unanswerable questions draining everyone's time. Today I told him that he's no longer allowed in the plant. I thought that's what you were calling about."

Fred simply said, "Nope."

"I guess if you flush enough down the toilet it comes out somewhere. Too bad it was on Jim," he thought.

He remembered when they had worked together on the construction of the Casanova Creek Site. The commode in the plant manager's office (big deal that it was back then) hadn't been working right. One night they did some re-plumbing together, and as it turned out inadvertently by-passed the water pressure regulator. After they valved the water back in, Jim said he'd give it a try. When he was done with his business, he gave the handle a kick as was his habit. It was as if he had unleashed an angry sea monster. The toilet blew back all its contents with the unregulated force of a 180 psi supply line. Jim stumbling back into the hallway screaming primeval vulgarities, totally drenched with however many gallons of water a 10 second burst of a 180 psi three quarter inch line could flow. Fred had started laughing and had to hang onto the wall in order not to fall.

Fred chuckled and asked Jim whether he remembered that night.

Jim started laughing, "I still tell that story – two trained professionals can screw up anything." That seemed to clear the air. Fred said, "Well now that we are both on the same page; I want to know what's going on. These Friday scud missile attacks have everyone running for cover. And worse . . . staying there."

"That's not totally true," Jim replied. "You missed the part about everyone firing back at each other. If one lands in my yard, I fire back. It's usually at sales or marketing. If I don't, I'd lose the respect of my organization."

The conversation just got worse and worse. Everyone feared everyone else. The organization had turned inward on itself and was in a constant feeding frenzy. Hypocrisy and cynicism were the new guiding principles. "How could it have gone so wrong? How do we get what we had back?" Fred mused.

Jim said, "I don't know. That's why you are getting paid the big bucks. I've got to go. It's Friday and we're losing daylight. I've got to launch some missiles."

And that was that. Inaction is a powerful "voice". By not cutting this behavior off, by allowing the adversarial free-for-all to grow unabated, and a zero-sum attitude to prevail, Cliff had focused and shaped organizational thinking from collaborators to internal competitors.

Cliff and his company had fallen into a common trap. Instead of maintaining the mindset and values that successfully launched his company, Cliff let it slowly morph into how companies of similar size operate – where organizational structure and turf rule. The simple protocol of conducting meetings set by the top management gets mimicked throughout organizations setting the tone and norm for how people interact.

Many of a company's stories have their origins in meetings, probably because the participants' actions and behavior are retold for emphasis and because meetings take up a significant amount of the workday.

Are meeting AIMs preannounced stating clearly what is to be accomplished in the meeting; how the meeting will be conducted; and inputs needed to accomplish the AIM? And why accomplishing the AIM is important? Are there rules of behavior for the meeting – engage and interact like allies or go after each other like a WWE Wrestlemania Cage Match? Are staff meetings held "just because?"

It's not that difficult to start creating new stories to begin reshaping an organization's thinking about how it should engage by simply changing the leadership meeting process and behaviors. Stories travel through an organization quicker than anything you can write or say, faster than Friday staff emails.

If You Are What You Eat, Your Company Is What It Thinks

    Restructuring staff meetings is a loud voice that will quickly be absorbed and emulated by an organization fundamentally changing its thinking.

If You Are What You Eat, Your Company Is What It Thinks

Chapter 3

"HARDWIRED"

Frank was either a genius or a lunatic. There is a thin line separating the two, or so they say. It depended on who you talked to. He was the real deal – brilliant by most standards. He had a passion for invention, and for the most part was able to develop these inventions into innovations. He had a driving sense of indestructibility.

Everywhere he turned he saw problems reaching out to him begging for solutions. Problems he and only he could solve. He knew that a business only exists to solve problems. If he could get the problem defined correctly there was a new business opportunity waiting. He was blessed with the tenacity to stay with a problem until he figured out what it all meant.

Frank was a fun guy – but it got exhausting when you were trapped with him in the confines of a car or plane. He just couldn't stop himself from adding his two cents about everything he saw. It didn't take long riding with him on the interstate before you could feel the "Who Cares" tractor beam pulling you in. Within an hour, you were so far into the "zone" that jumping out of the car at high speed seemed like a sensible choice.

He always drove – go figure. Idle hands are the devil's workshop, but after an hour with his mind you knew Satan. How many ways can you make a billboard any better – and who on earth is going to put up with radio pop-up ads every time you pass a billboard!

Internet pop-ups are a scourge – on the other hand interstate radio pop-ups would spur an entire new industry – radio pop-up blocking. Create the technology for billboard radio pop-ups – then create the technology to block it. That's how he thought.

Allan Odell had a great advertising idea with his "pop-up" Burma Shave signs. From 1925 to well into the '60's they were an icon. Before DVD players for backseat passengers, there wasn't a whole lot a parent could do beyond license plate bingo and the alphabet game. Spotting Burma Shave signs would stop any back seat quarreling in its tracks. It was something a parent could count on.

But President Eisenhower did in 'Burma Shave' signs with the creation of the interstate system. You can't read anything at those speeds having lettering less than three feet high without getting into an accident.

You had to admire Frank, a brilliant mind, even though it was totally warped from time to time. What makes a mind like that click? Not a woman. He had a lot of good women behind him, so to speak. He had been through multiple wives and was working on his next live-in. Nobody ever heard much about the breakups, but knowing how his mind worked, it is a wonder one of these women hadn't done him serious harm. A mental picture of Frank making love and jabbering was comic relief. Owning a business and his whole invincible persona made up the magnetic force that drew women toward him. But the force that repelled women was the litany of simple things – everything could be better. He wanted everyone to know he had a better notion – including his significant others. It wasn't so much that he was a male chauvinist pig. He wasn't. Truthfully he just couldn't help himself, it's just who he was.

What was true in his personal life was true in his business life. The brilliance of his mind initially overcame the cold blanket of his behavior. He set the "difficult person" standard. His genius attracted people to work for him. His behavior caused them to leave. He just couldn't hunker down and simply listen. He always had to be right – the exclusive domain of college professors. If he stumbled into a conversation at work, his instant response was "I guess this requires an executive decision!" and he'd tell everyone what to do and how to do it – end of discussion.

He wasn't exactly a control freak – he just needed to be in control. He knew what he wanted and wanted what he knew to the exclusion of everything else. But that had its limitations. His company had been around for years – it beat the survival odds, a testimony to his innovative genius. It had provided him a lifestyle and recognition.

But his business wasn't sound. If you looked at the revenue stream, at first glance you'd say it was seasonally cyclical. But when you looked at the timeline you saw that the cycle was about three years. A sustained healthy rise followed by a precipitous collapse. So your next guess might justifiably be a product life cycle S-curve. If you dug a little deeper, you found that the revenue drop-off had nothing to do with the maturity of the product – he was always innovating and improving the product line. What you would find is the immediate cause in each death cycle was the loss of key people.

But why? It's too simple to say that people hated him – although many ended up that way. He was a good guy – annoying to the point of tears at times, but we all have that potential. And it wasn't that he didn't care about people – he genuinely did. In the final analysis you would find that he was a line of sight, command and control person. Out of sight wasn't out of mind. But out of sight was a loss of control.

Frank grappled with that issue, but he could never bring himself to let go – let someone else carry the ball. He had this fear that people just wouldn't do what needed to be done – right being the way he thought best how to do it – and that changed situationally. At any given time, 'right' was up for grabs, because every time you asked him, he'd "improve" on his last answer.

If you like a company where you want to be told what to do every time something needs doing; and one where you never have to think, this was the place. It gave you a lot of free time waiting for Frank to get back to you. And there was a core group of hanger-ons who liked just that.

But then, there were those who didn't. To be good, a salesperson has to have a healthy streak of greed; and be driven to win. When Frank got crosswise with a salesperson's cash flow, good things would not happen. Every salesperson covets "their way". When someone starts fooling around with a salesperson's "way" it just doesn't sit well. He knew that without someone to sell the solutions he came up with, his innovations would be downgraded to mere inventions collecting cobwebs in the US Patent Office archives.

Frank had a bad habit of making a customer wrong. If the customer didn't get that they were wrong right away – Frank kept pounding them until they admitted it, or they threw him out. So he needed people who could sell and make the customer right even when they were wrong. He couldn't. His mind got in the way. He was humble in that regard – he saw that reality and accepted it – he stunk as a salesman. So he put together one of the sweetest pay packages any salesperson could ever dream of – it was the ultimate "honey pot". It was just too much for any salesperson worth their salt to resist. But everything comes at a price.

The net result of all this was a company bounded by the capacity of Frank's mental processing ability and his physical ability to overcome the obstacles of time and space. You can't be everywhere at the same time – although he was working on improving that – a Smartphone was a start – if it just wasn't for losing the darn thing!

If you think about the way the thinking processes operated in the company, Frank was the CPU, and everyone else was hardwired to it. As the business grew, the CPU went into overload. When the CPU was overloaded – everything slowed down. When a salesperson couldn't make "the deal," well that got ugly – he was cutting off their money pipeline – if you don't close – you don't get paid. The money pipeline gets blocked; the salesperson isn't happy. When a salesperson isn't happy – nothing gets sold.

The 3-year cycle of collapse could be traced back in each case to a triggering event. The trigger was always an annual sales meeting. Once a year, Frank would have all the field sales people come to the mothership to have their "morale boosted." Ironic how it always worked out. After about three years, the newbies had morphed into cynical 'old hands.' His "never good enough" and "wait for me to decide" or "I'll decide" aura was tolerable as a new hire salesperson, but was now intolerable.

He had good intentions. Frank knew salespeople were a prerequisite to business success, and they ought to be happy. Happy for a salesperson meant only one thing – money. To motivate, he would always tinker with the salesperson's compensation system before each meeting, and then use the meeting to announce the changes. To his credit, in all cases the changes were for the betterment of the salesperson. But the change was always so convoluted that even accounting couldn't explain it clearly, and that left the salesforce assuming about anything they wanted – which was always the worst.

And so every three years – like clockwork – there were mass resignations from the sales staff – sometimes whole geographic regions – usually decided over drinks at the hotel bar where the sales meeting was being held. There was always a valiant effort to hang on to territory and customer relationships – but the "wait 'til Frank tells us" core that was left behind was just too slow to deal with the abrupt loss of customer access. The customers' doors opened wide and in came the competitors. In most cases led by the salespeople who had just left – so much for trade secrets law and ethics. To some people, any behavior was a justified response to Frank's behavior.

His business' destiny was ordained. The way his thinking was hardwired, so too was the company's thinking. And, because his mental "wiring" only had a finite capability, so too did his business. Frank's business was forever locked in a cycle of rising up to the capacity of his CPU – and then collapsing back. His business was bounded by what he could think. At the bottom of each crash, Frank always placed the blame elsewhere – he never looked in the mirror.

Command and control management style is something we learn from our parents. For those of us who have raised children, we know the hardest part is letting go. From letting go on their first solo steps, to taking the training wheels off their bike and launching them to freedom; to giving them the car keys to run that first errand for you; to keeping your mouth shut while twenty-something's are finding their way. It's hard because you care so much. But just as children learn their parents values and sense of purpose, so do the organizations and the people you lead. If your organization can only act when you are riding shotgun, it caps what an organization can be and do.

Letting go can begin simply with chartering a task team, documenting the purpose of the team, defining how members will work, and expected outcomes. There are templates for team chartering that establish the bounds of freedom and order as well as feedback channels when the going gets tough. These templates ask questions that are uncomfortable for the person whose comfort zone is command and control.

Feeling the discomfort and pushing through it starts the voyage of personal change. Once you get comfortable with team chartering you can expand to ever widening circles of concern and eventually reframe the company ethos. And isn't a charter another name for a business plan? Does the organization or team you lead or are a member of have a charter?

If You Are What You Eat, Your Company Is What It Thinks

Chapter 4

"THE DREADED CUSTOMER"

George was a good old boy in the Southern tradition. His nickname growing up was "Cooter." He'd acquired it when he came down with a bad case of the zits crossing over into manhood. His friends said his face looked like the back of a painted turtle when he had his zit cream on and christened him Cooter. Not that this had much to do with anything. But it did force him to have a quick sense of humor. That was the best remedy he could come up with after hearing his Mom recite the "sticks and stones" thing for the umpteenth time.

George had started out with a company in sales shortly after flunking out of an infamous party school. He didn't quite get the part where showing up for class and taking tests was a required part of the curriculum. By his first semester junior year, he thought he was beyond that, but that's not how his professors saw it. In addition to the "book learning," college prepared him with exceptional people skills, a requisite for success in the world of business. That was something he hadn't quite mastered back in his "Cooter days". Sort of the opposite. Albeit his learning in college came mostly at parties and bars, but practice makes perfect. And George got a lot of practice in his tenure in college.

George leveraged what he had learned at school and moved up the corporate ladder from an inside customer service rep, to VP of sales – a sterling accomplishment. George learned how to make a business friend. He never sold anything – people bought him. Build a relationship. That was his "way." And it was a good approach. That wasn't always the case.

When he moved to his first outside sales assignment, he found out a push selling strategy the company taught just wasn't going to cut it. It just wasn't the 'Southern Way.' One night after a futile day of "selling", George was sitting at a bar watching the crowd, when in walked Sal, a prospect he had talked with earlier in the day. He was being escorted by a competitor. He remembered the guy's name was Bernie from the "other" company. He'd seen his name on the visitor's sign in sheet when he was checking out at reception and as Bernie was the only visitor signed in after him and he'd seen him in the waiting area near Sal's office it must be him. That deductive sleuthing gave George a flush of confidence.

Bernie and Sal were seated at a table carrying on like long lost fraternity brothers. George just sat there and watched; nursing his bar rail blended scotch (his boss had told him to acquire a taste for scotch). So when Bernie left with Sal, George quietly followed. Their next stop was a strip club down the street. George slithered in and found a seat where he could watch from the shadows.

Bernie kept a handle on Sal – "no touch nothing to tell" approach. George made a note of that. The evening ended about 9:30 with Bernie seeing Sal off. George tailed Bernie back to the hotel bar where all sales people go before retiring. George went up to the bar and plopped next to Bernie. Bernie turned to him and told George he

If You Are What You Eat, Your Company Is What It Thinks

wouldn't make much of a spy. He also recited George's complete bio (including his last semester in college).

George was astonished. He'd always thought himself pretty darn good about being visibly invisible. And who the heck was this guy, knowing everything about him. So George fell back on his college people skills training and offered to buy Bernie a drink. Now any salesperson will tell you their favorite kind of drink is "free." So Bernie obliged and ordered himself a top-shelf single malt scotch.

George felt his face going red. Luckily he hadn't eaten anything for dinner yet. There would be no way he could bury the cost of Bernie's drink in the expense account if he had a meal too. So they got talking, and one thing led to another. Bernie said, "I'll give you some pointers about sales. The first being it's a whole lot easier to get a friend to buy from you, than an enemy. The second is that if you're going to have a friend, you better know everything about them down to the dental floss they use."

George pondered that for a moment or two, and then asked how it was Bernie knew so much about him, because he sure didn't see Bernie as wanting to be a friend or sell him anything. So Bernie explained as he polished off his top-shelf single-malt and got up to leave, that competitors were different – you needed to know them better than a friend. George had a laugh, and said as Bernie was leaving that he hadn't told him which dental floss he used. To which Bernie replied, "You don't floss," and left. And that was the start of George's ascension to the top. Don't sell – make a friend. Let them buy you.

Now George had a dry sense of humor. On his way up the ladder George had this wry quip for when things weren't going just right. When a discussion came to an imponderable end, George would always dryly joke "The dreaded customer." Those in sales knew that it was a comic break. They also knew that quip meant to get to work – a subtle push from George that they hadn't done their homework.

Early on George learned that doing the jiggle bar circuit wasn't a real key to a business friendship, which was a bit of a disappointment to him. He learned that you never did anything that might jeopardize a "friend's" job by putting them in a situation where if it became known, their job might be at risk. He also learned that getting to know everything about a person wasn't about blackmailing them.

Friendship was about caring for someone and their problems. So George quit selling. He set out to be a trusted friend. The buying came later. It was like ivy. After you plant it, the first year it sleeps, the second it creeps, and the third year it leaps. It didn't take too many years for his business friendships to leap. And it wasn't long for his career to follow suit.

But nobody had clued George into the role of senior management. Nobody ever told George that people would hang on every word he said, and then watch his every action to learn what he meant. It's not like he missed it in school; they don't teach it there. The place it's usually learned is at the plant site, typically at zero dark thirty when you earn the respect of someone with whom you're working to get a production line running – and they'll tell you. Well, George had gone the straight sales career track. He'd walked through plant sites to get to shipping or the scheduler's office, but he had never worked there.

If You Are What You Eat, Your Company Is What It Thinks

Now the sales force knew what George meant when he flipped the phrase "the dreaded customer." They saw George in action. The words were in stark contrast to his actions – but that was okay – George was a fun guy. They understood.

But the people who were in operations at the plant sites never saw George in the field with the customers. He was a great people person, and everyone enjoyed being near him. He had developed this flamboyant bigger than life air about him. They heard what he said and took what he said to heart. People paid attention when he spoke.

George realized that the future lay with getting everyone to know the customer. In all the years of operation, this company had never sent a manufacturing person out to see a customer – not even a plant manager much less an operator. The company had thrived on the stovepipe approach – adversarial relationships bring out the best was the credo.

George had a vision – if the person who used the material he was selling, were also a friend of the person inside making it – voila! The perfect storm! So he set out to do just that – the "Make-a-Friend" program launched with George carrying the flag. There were posters, tee-shirts, mugs, and the whole shebang. George was feeling great – like the boy who stuck in his thumb and pulled out a plum.

But cynicism was a deeply embedded part of the company. Even George – albeit a great guy – was looked at with a jaundiced eye. Everyone outside the close-knit sales group looked at this "Make-a-Friend" program with trepidation. After all, it was George himself that mothered the "Dreaded Customer" to full term. It had become the mantra of manufacturing every time a product complaint was received.

A late delivery complaint was shrugged off by distribution as the "Dreaded Customer." Research and Development looked at customers with disdain – they just didn't understand. The "Dreaded Customer" fit a comfortable mental framework. The Comptroller was always squeezing budgets. Customer programs and travel expense were always the first to feel the pinch. To the CEO and the VP of Operations it was all bottom-line – "ship it." Unless goodwill can be turned into a receivable in 30 days – it is a waste – and by golly "we mean to be lean." So the phrase George had coined –the "Dreaded Customer" easily fit.

The VP of Ops and the CFO went along with the "Friend" thing. They all competed for the same money pool that George did – let him walk the plank, and we'll cut it off was a part of the managerial tradition – "kept everyone on their toes" you see.

After only one week from the launch of the "Make a Friend" program, George got his first whiff that something was wasn't going well. It caught him like the smell of a dead armadillo that had baked out in the sun on the side of the road. Why was it that these critters seemed always to die with their feet straight up – and their front paws folding together in prayer? Who was the first redneck to discover that the distance between a dead armadillo's snout and their front paws was the perfect fit for cradling a longneck beer bottle?

So George went to find his friend Bill in purchasing. He and Bill had been a pair back in the day. They had chased around town during mating season that had been a 24/7 activity back then. They had formed the company softball team together, and they made sure there was always ice available for bumps and contusions incurred during each game. The ice also hid the beer. George found Bill, and they went to lunch. George got to the point – "What the heck is going on?" And Bill was equally direct. He explained to George that he had set himself up.

"What are you talking about?"

"Welcome to the game of inside politics. You've been out in the field so long you just don't get it – do you? Look, politics is a zero-sum game. If you're winning, someone else is losing. I know you, and I have known for years what you meant by your "Dreaded Customer" crack. But everyone else took you literally."

"You've got to be kidding me. What are you talking about and what politics?"

"Nope, I'm not kidding. And George, you're the golden boy around here. Whether you like it or not you are. You got the Board's attention. You deliver. You are a threat not only to your peers who are eyeing upward mobility, but also to the CEO. Politics, good grief you're naïve. You've become too successful. When you were out in the field, everyone and anyone could take credit. But now that you're on corporate staff, well the Board isn't stupid. Do you think the CEO brought you in? And now that you're here, you aren't going to get much help – except maybe an ample supply of rope to hang yourself with."

And with that, their lunch arrived. Looking at his plate of food, George got a mental picture of himself as an armadillo, the CFO a truck that was determined to run him over, and the VP of Ops ready to plant a longneck beer bottle in-between his paws. Everybody was not on board with the politically correct "the customer is always right." The "dreaded customer" from George was a comment that had landed on fertile ground.

If You Are What You Eat, Your Company Is What It Thinks

Redemption eventually came, but it took time and energy as the organization began to see firsthand George interacting with customers – his "voice." You don't get rid of kudzu easily, and neither can you get rid of the effects a senior manager's flip remark and the impact it has on an organization's perception and thinking. The "dreaded customer" was a loud bell that drew immediate attention. It focused blame away from the organization's accountability, which was very easy to swallow. George's "voice" had been silent to the majority of the organization who never saw him with customers until he took the additional steps of engaging with them.

Like any leader, every word matters but clarity is only gained through a leader's observed actions. Management actions, good or bad, build into stories. These stories mushroom into legends that shape and guide the organization's thinking. They are the foundation of Corporate Think that people use in dealing with the myriad of daily dilemmas and interactions where there is no management presence to direct them.

Chapter 5

"YES WE CAN"

My cynical side reacted with a visceral flinch. The phrase was coming from a DVD my grandchildren were playing in the other room. How preposterous to be indoctrinating children in a positive attitude. How dare we raise expectations?

Why is it so easy to get cynical? Why are cynical characters in the media, from the movies to nightly news talking heads, so easy to side with? Why do we automatically jump to the side of a skeptic? Is this because there is no risk in being a skeptic? Self-preservation is a basic instinct we all possess. Maybe that's what it's all about. Survival! Cynicism is instinctual, embedded in whatever it is that defines us. Cynicism may be God's special gift to us. It stops us from throwing ourselves off cliffs, even though flying would be cool.

Take Wally. He seemed to lack that instinctual code. He had jumped off a few figurative cliffs. He'd come onto a great idea and then just couldn't help himself from taking the leap.

When Wally was a boy of 12, he came up with the idea that a tall cold glass of lemonade, spiked with a splash of his dad's vodka, would sell on a hot summer day. So he set up a stand on the front lawn and did it. Everything went great until Wally's mom looked out the window and saw the crowd of teenage boys in the front yard.

Wally's mom was a good mom. And like all good moms she knew what she saw just wasn't right. How do moms know anyhow? In addition to being grounded, Wally had to put all the money he made in the church collection basket the following Sunday. Not the best ending as Wally saw it. But he learned.

Wally's next venture was to convince his friend Tim that the old wrapping paper and balsa stick contraption that Wally glued together in the garage would let Tim fly if he jumped off a dog house roof. Wally learned he was pretty good at marketing and sales, which was simply getting people to "yes". By the age of 12 or 13, you've got the basic reasoning skills in place to see you through life, although a boy's testosterone usually kicks in around that age too. Testosterone gives men the dubious advantage of being able to act without thinking.

Whether it was Wally's emerging marketing skills or Tim's emerging testosterone, Tim got to "yes" and with a primeval whoop, leapt off the roof of the doghouse, immediately landing in the pyracantha firethorn surrounding it. The firethorn broke the fall leaving Tim with no head injuries or broken bones. But the thorns had done a number on Tim. He was already whimpering when Wally hauled him out of the bush.

When Wally got him out, he could see blood streaming everywhere. That caused Wally to scream – that in turn caused Tim to scream. The screams were infectious. Wally's screams fed on Tim's screams and vice versa.

Wally's mom was the next on the scene. She took one look at the two of them, both with their white tee-shirts covered in blood, and she screamed. It didn't take long for the neighborhood posse to assemble. But it did take a good long while for the communal screaming to stop.

Wally learned another powerful lesson that day. First, he wasn't cut out to be a doctor like his mom wanted. The sight of blood was more than he could handle. Second, there is a path to get to what you want, and the first step is not leap. A leap in faith and leap into action are different matters entirely.

The antithesis of cynicism is naiveté. Now naiveté is for sure how we all start life. We can easily observe it in children and puppies. But we can just as easily watch it dissolve away.

One can make a very reasoned argument that cynicism is not some genetic thing, but a learned behavior. It's a conditioned response. One isn't born on the dark side; one is turned to it. Maybe the turning point was when grandpa got you for the third time with the pull his finger trick. Or when your friends at school told you there was no Easter bunny and had a good laugh at your expense (so what if you're 16).

Naiveté never totally disappears. It lurks under the surface waiting to be set free. The key to unleashing it is probably hope, the hope that something is true. On the other hand the pain of embarrassment, humiliation, disappointment keeps it under the surface. Being for something is an uphill battle against the cynics who have to expend very little energy throwing marbles of doubt on the floor under your feet.

Wally went on to college – although not through Pre-Med like his mom had wanted. He did take one semester though. It was when he went to the Pre-Med Club's evening get together which started out with a video on surgery. Wally passed out cold two minutes into it.

If You Are What You Eat, Your Company Is What It Thinks

Next semester Wally made the jump to engineering. His curiosity and "why not" attitude kept his grades down – in engineering school there is only one text book answer, probably more for grading purposes. When you get out in the real world you find there is no singular answer because you never have all the information to plug into the equations that you were a slave to in college.

Wally did well enough with his grades that he was able to hook up with a good company at graduation. He soon discovered that "Can DO" attitudes, while appreciated, always got the wet blanket of "we already tried that" or "that won't work". But, Wally persevered. Over 5-years, he had some embarrassing flops, but he also had some good successes.

On the day that he received his five-year service award, it was like the lights flickered for an instant. What Wally saw frightened him. He wasn't in a tunnel going somewhere – he was in a cave! That night, he put his epiphany into words. He explained to his bride of two years who was six months pregnant what he must do. Swimming upstream for five years against the flow of cynicism had taken its toll. It was killing him. So they came up with a plan. He would get the company to turn over the rights of a patent he had been granted that the company had no interest in pursuing. Then they'd go to the entrepreneur's best allies – the 3-F's – Family, Friends, and Fools. They'd start a business out of their garage.

In addition to money, Wally found some good coaches, mentors and advisors. It took a few years, but they made it. Wally founded and built his company around the notion of "Yes we can!" It was the overriding principle of the corporate tradition he nurtured and grew. The one thing Wally never wanted to see again was the constant struggle of swimming against the open floodgates of cynicism.

Wally had pictured his business as a boat – and who hasn't. A boat is a popular business metaphor. Sure the engine room is manufacturing, and fuel is customers (who pay), and the compass is marketing. But once people get through the analysis of the metaphor as it applies to their organization, they quickly start jousting for position.

The carcass of a dead cow floating down a flooded river is a "boat". No sane person would be fighting over deckchairs on a dead bloated cow whose only propulsion is the flatulence brought on by morbidity. But it's hard to see your business as a dead cow until it erupts with a room clearing stench and roar, starts breaking up, and heads for the bottom. Staying in a state of denial is a comforting way to be.

But Wally took the boat idea to the next level. He saw ideas as new, small boats. He saw cynicism and skepticism as torpedoes and turbulent waters. Sure it may look and smell like cow, but whatever. He saw the role of people in the organization as not to elbow for position at the deck rails to watch and see, and to take turns pissing over the side to see if they can hit the new boat. A new boat is fragile. It needs protection. It needs support. It sure doesn't need a "golden shower".

Wally saw people's role in the organization as jumping in the water and helping keep a new boat afloat. If everyone put their energy into making a new boat work and survive there was a much better hope of good outcomes. If with everyone focused on keeping it afloat and making it seaworthy, at some point it would either do and be that or, everyone including the idea's owner would see and understand why it never would.

When Wally hired he always screened for not so much naiveté, but a glimmer of it under the surface of the candidates. Wally found that surrounding a person with a positive attitude – a can do attitude – could be perceived as equally perilous to some as the cynical environment Wally had fled from.

People came into the company enthused by the energy they discovered during the interview process. It was in sharp contrast to where they had been. Some jumped in and thrived. But others just couldn't handle being surrounded by optimism and the charge to "go make a difference". A new hire's personal revelation occurred quickly. They would get swept away in the spirit of the place and toss out an idea that the first time it passed through their brain was after it has escaped their mouth and reentered through their ears.

Shock and awe when people chimed in with words like "great idea!" and "go-for-it!" They were hit with a gigantic wave of optimism breaking over their heads. People honestly expected them to pick up the flag and jump into their "boat". What they did from there on out determined whether they stayed or not. Those whose core skill was attending meetings, quickly fled in horror. But then there were those that took the leap and thrived.

Wally recognized there was magic in bold ideas. Bold ideas had a way of capturing people's attention and energy. As Wally's business grew, he did understand that there was the inevitable reality of having to deal with the minutiae of growing a great idea and supporting it with the mundane daily chores of sales, service, manufacturing, collections, ordering, and all the other stuff that pumps money into a company. He also understood that he didn't have to deal with it; he could hire people who could.

But he believed that anyone in the organization, even if their role was mundane, ought to have and be able to express new ideas – launch new boats. Wally kept up the hiring filter for everyone, regardless of where they were in the organization. Finding purchasing agents and buyers, and worse yet accountants that weren't cynical turned out to be a daunting task – but doable in the end.

Wally's business grew with leaps and bounds. He kept it private. Stock market gurus were the worse. They earned their living on cynicism. He stayed with traditional banking. Growth creates this tremendous sucking sound, often referred to in business circles as cash. Wally worked the loan covenants, and that was that.

But that didn't keep the stock market gurus at bay as Wally's company grew – and Wally grew older. It turned out they were the best advertising one could ask for. They kept everyone watching. The speculation around what would happen when Wally retired, and worst yet the one jerk kept using the term "when Mr. Wally dies".

But Wally knew he had built something special. Sure everyone would miss him when he left. But the spirit and thinking grounded in CAN DO was now so deeply embedded in what Wally's company was, that it would never die without a serious fight.

Wally built one final twist into the plan for his transition. The family would continue to own the company, but they would not run it. His replacement and all the replacements of senior staff would be based on a selection process run like that Idol thing (which Wally didn't much care for) or the Tribe thing (which Wally cared less for). But Wally loved the idea of voting people on, off, in or whatever.

Wally trusted everyone who was a part of his company – now how weird is that! Wally always went to sleep with a smile. "Just wait until people see my transition plan. What a great idea!"

Continual reinforcement of organizational thought processes is an everyday, without exception affair. Constancy of purpose is communicated and engrained in organizational thinking through management's constancy of actions. It can be shaken through thoughtless actions, but once it is in place and supported with consistent management actions it becomes the DNA of Corporate Think. Contrary to some beliefs, people are always paying attention.

Chapter 6

"BUT . . ."

"Butt, butt, turkey butts." My kids used to run around shouting that phrase Thanksgiving morning to the horror of my mother when she visited. The world had changed from when my mother raised me and my siblings. Back then a stern reprimand with a swift spank to the fanny got things right. The same action is now borderline child abuse. Although we had grown up unscathed (or so we thought) there are extremes that need to stop.

When my wife and I were raising our kids, for the most part we went with the "point out the behavior that is not acceptable, explain, and use logic" route. And for the most part, it didn't work. With our kids, you were guaranteed to get, "But Dad lets me!" (A big fat lie – well maybe); or "But Mom!" When they discovered the word "Whatever" it was a game changer, a word that goes right through flesh and hits parental bone.

Words matter. The word "but" in the business world can be a precursor to doubt, confrontation, or optimism. It is a word with no boundaries. It can be used in talking about the past, present, or future. It can introduce a game ender, or the start of a whole new conversation. It can mean a new beginning or the beginning of the end. It can be imploring or reassuring. "But" is just that kind of word.

Sam found himself in a company that thrived on "buts". Where Sam worked, "but" was usually used in the same phrase with the word "considered". Sam became very "but" conscious. He wasn't sure if it was a mental tic or what. He just seemed to hear every single "but", and had a hard time not discounting everything that came after it.

Now, there is nothing more polite and reaffirming than knowing people have been listening to you. And a tactic that had become a habit was for people to state back to the speaker what they'd just heard. The word "but" was a trigger word for the practice. "I hear you, but . . ."

Sam found himself struggling to keep up with conversations in meetings. Every "but" was a mental detour for him. He had to do something. It was driving him batty. Sam quickly learned that meetings here never got anywhere. They never got you fired either.

So he decided to keep track of the number of "buts" uttered in a meeting. After the first meeting, he had counted seventeen. He looked at the number and felt vindicated.

Sam realized the raw number was just not enough with which to confront his coworkers. He also noticed meetings always seemed to end in a flurry of buts. Over the course of the next two weeks, Sam plotted the number of buts versus the elapsed time in the meeting.

When he dumped the data into a spreadsheet and added a trendline, the R factor was 0.91 for an exponential relationship over the course of the meeting. He imported the equation into an audio software package on his home computer, then recorded a sound bite of himself saying "but", did a little wizardry, and hit play.

If You Are What You Eat, Your Company Is What It Thinks

The noise coming out of his computer's speakers sounded like a Geiger counter closing in on a nuclear warhead. But . . . . . . But . . . . But . . . But . . But . But.But.But.But.But.

Now the question was what to do with it. Sam took a copy on a flash drive into work the next day. Sam's instincts were good, but he often ignored them when it came to women and office protocol. So he sent it to Carol with a short explanation of its origin. He sort-of-kinda had this thing about her, and he figured this would impress her. Sam had the presence of mind to ask Carol not to forward his email.

It wasn't too long before he heard his Geiger counter going off in a cubical in the general direction of where Carol sat. "Too cool," Sam thought to himself. "Maybe catch Carol later and ask her out for a little socializing after work." Sam took off for a meeting feeling pretty good. An hour later when he returned, he plopped back down at his desk and checked his email. "A note from Carol, ta-dah!" Sam thought.

Before he could get it open, a familiar sound came not from the direction where Carol sat, but an entirely different direction. Sam's ears perked up. Maybe he was just dreaming. There it was again from another direction. Sam's jaw dropped. "Holy Cow!" Within minutes the floor came alive with what sounded like a choral society of toads after a rain storm. But . . . . . . But . . . . But . . . But . . But . But.But.But.But.But.

Sam wasn't an idiot. He knew he was screwed. As he dialed Carol's number, he swore he'd never do something that stupid again. Of course, that oath was meaningless – that wasn't going to happen.

"Carol!!"

If You Are What You Eat, Your Company Is What It Thinks

"Hi Sam! Cool soundtrack!"

"Glad you liked it. Did you forward my email to anyone?"

"Of course not. I did save the soundtrack and sent it to a few friends though."

Sam felt a bit of relief. As long as he was off the email chain he figured he had dodged a bullet. With renewed confidence Sam said, "Hey, do you want to get together right after work for a beer over at Charlie's 134 Grille?"

"Sure. How about I meet you there at 5:30?"

"Great!! See you there."

"No pain no gain" Sam chortled. "You just got to put yourself out there now and again." Later on in his career Sam would use this event to differentiate the huge dissimilarity between taking a chance and managing a risk.

As Sam came back into the conscious world, he again heard the ongoing chorus of butting rippling through the room. He laughed to himself and went back to work. But then like an electric jolt, his mind snapped to attention. The "butting" had suddenly stopped. Now in nature that means only one thing. Something higher up on the food chain had entered the room. The sudden quiet sent a chill down his spine. Sam didn't hear any death rattles so after awhile he figured whatever had happened it didn't involve him.

At 5:35 Sam met up with Carol and the evening went great, and he totally forgot about his "but" audio going office viral. The next morning when Sam got to work there was a buzz going on by the coffee pot. Sam sauntered over to find out that the soundtrack had made its way to the CEO; and that the CEO had unleashed his executive assistant to find the culprit.

Sam's life flashed before his face. He felt like he was drowning. Now anyone who has been around knows a CEO's executive assistant is not someone to fool with. They know more about what's going on than the cumulative knowledge of the organization.

It was at that point Sam remembered. If you clicked the properties on the file, it would give the author up. He'd forgotten to expunge his name that was automatically attached when he created the file. If he got caught was no longer in play. It was just a matter of when. At that moment, Sam decided to go for broke. Sam went back to his desk, grabbed the data that he had used to create the soundtrack, and sat there waiting for the inevitable.

It didn't take long. Sam's boss came in and said he'd just been called by the executive assistant, and they were wanted in the senior staff meeting NOW! Sam's boss was excited. He'd never been summoned to an executive committee meeting. "A turning point in both our careers," he said to Sam as they hustled down the hall to the elevator.

Sam wasn't saying anything as they marched toward the briar patch. He figured he might as well let him go to the gallows with a smile on his face. They arrived and after a short wait they were ushered in.

The first signal that caught his boss's attention was that there were no empty chairs. So they just stood.

The CEO signaled to the media booth at the other end of the room and said "I want you two clowns to listen to this." Sam could

If You Are What You Eat, Your Company Is What It Thinks

sense his boss shudder. The continuous "butting" loop began. After what seemed to be an eternity the CEO waved to the media booth to cut it off.

The CEO said, "I'd like an explanation." Sam took a sideward glance at his boss who had now put a good five feet between them. The Senior VP of HR, who legend had it, only spoke up when the outcome was a sure thing said, "We don't need an explanation." The CEO cut him off. "You may not need an explanation but I do!"

Sam took another look for his boss and saw him now fully wedged in the conference room corner. "Dang!" was the only thing that came into Sam's mind. But then to his surprise he heard his voice. He heard himself explaining how his boss had shared with him the CEO's concern about the seeming lack of speed the organization was able to muster in implementing anything anymore. How he'd used his Green Belt training on process measurement to analyze meeting productivity; and how he had settled in on the use of the word "but" to track it, and that the use of the word "but" in the discussion was an indicator of hesitation.

Sam glanced over at his boss who was now looking ashen jammed in the corner. Sam continued that he had collected, analyzed, and determined the correlation between elapsed meeting time and the use of the word "but." He finished by saying that he had shared this with several people trying to build support for a Six Sigma project, and he regretted its premature release to such a broad audience.

Utter silence. The CEO just stared at Sam. CEO's are exceptional practitioners of poker faces. And Sam's CEO was no exception. Sam glanced around the room again. His boss was still crammed in the corner. He did notice a subtle grin on the COO's face. The Senior VP of HR was still stone-faced and indignant.

The CEO asked Sam and his boss to wait outside, with which they gratefully complied. After a short wait, the conference room door opened. The first out was the Senior VP of HR, an Irishman whose facial veins gave no doubt about his feelings. This guy was pissed – not good Sam thought. The complexion of Sam's boss had just reverted back to ashen.

The COO was next out, and he gave Sam a wink and a grin. "REDEMPTION," Sam thought, "Was it possible?"

The executive assistant asked Sam to step back inside, and told Sam's boss he could go back downstairs. Sam glanced at his boss and thought he saw an expanding wet patch on his khaki pants as he walked jerkily out of the reception area. Sam went back into the conference room. It was just he and the CEO. Everyone else was gone.

The CEO spoke. "I'll tell you right now, that what you did is not the accepted way of doing things around here. When there are issues, there are ways to deal with them. You have embarrassed me and my staff. We have become the laughing-stock of this company."

"Oh CRAP!!!" screamed in Sam's head. His lips went dry, and he felt he should swallow, but he just couldn't.

The CEO asked, "What do you have to say?"

Again, Sam heard himself talking, "This isn't good" he said in a meek voice.

"Do Ya think Sam?" the CEO said with a touch of sarcasm, but also a garnish of humor. "How you went about this sure isn't good. But then again, I don't know how you'd approach the 'emperor' and tell him he isn't wearing any clothes. We used to be a company that made decisions and were known for our speed. We're now a company known for our hesitation. Your 'but' thing does tell a story. Somewhere along the way we got it into our corporate heads that this ritualistic 'but' crap was healthy. We fell in love with meetings, not the reason for why we needed to meet. We fell in love with 'further review' and not getting into the water and managing a risk. Don't ever do something like this again – but, thanks for doing it."

The next day, the CEO set off on a two-week swing through the company talking with everyone, first in small groups, and then one-on-one. At the start of each group session, he played Sam's recording. He spoke of the company they had become and the company they needed to get back to being. He did give Sam credit for bringing this to his attention, and reiterated the need for critical thinking to flow more quickly in the future. The CEO's recognition of Sam brought more than a bit of attention Sam's way, including Carol's.

Listen for the repetitive words and phrases, the buzz in your organizations. For better or for worse they are shorthand for Corporate Think and the result of interpreting management actions.

Words and phrases rumbling through a company mean something. They flag organic corporate thought. "Spot on" – right?

If You Are What You Eat, Your Company Is What It Thinks

Chapter 7

"MAVERICKS"

Harry loved hiking. It fit his persona as an unbranded independent, adventuresome, free spirited kind of guy. Getting away from the constrictions of the everyday was an elixir. There was a certain rush that Harry could only find out on the trail.

Harry decided to take Sherry with him one Saturday. He'd met Sherry at a singles event where he found out she was an avid hiker too. He picked a hiking trail that was relatively easy so chatting was maximized and gasping for breath minimized. The purpose of the hike was to impress her not run each other into the ground.

The hike out went great. Sherry set a quick pace that impressed Harry. When they got to the waterfalls, which he had planned as the turnaround point, they were a bit behind on time – too much chatting. Getting back before dark might be close. As the thought of just turning around and heading back was forming in his head, Sherry stripped down to her undies and waded into the pool below the waterfalls.

Logical thinking vanished. Harry did the same and dove into the water. Harry couldn't recall how much time went by before Sherry scampered out of the water sounding the alarm "Snakes"!!!

Harry looked around and sure enough, there were three of them in the pool now. "They're copperheads!" Sherry shouted. Now Harry knew that wasn't likely to be true. They looked like northern water snakes. But then again, Sherry was an experienced hiker.

So Harry scrambled out. Sherry grinned and said, "Gotcha!"

After Harry had gotten his hiking gear back on, he looked up and realized they were in trouble. The sun was getting low. The trip back wasn't the best. The trail followed the stream and at points you were a step away from a precipitous freefall into space. In places, the mountain laurel made a tunnel that you could only pass through bent over at the waist. Harry always imagined running into a bear in one of those tangles. Not the best thought.

Harry set a quick pace in the failing light. That worried Sherry a bit, but Harry oozed confidence so Sherry fell in behind him. Harry finished the trail – daring but not reckless. Mavericks are often more fun to watch than join. Sherry was a kindred spirit. Harry had found his match. Mission accomplished.

The future is a dark place, but you keep on moving with what you've got, and Harry had this need to be free. Being penned in wasn't his cup of tea. Staying with the herd where the future was more a certainty gave him mental hives. If he were going over a cliff, it would be following his guidance system.

He had been lucky and fitted the mold where he worked. The hiring screens were set to sort out those who were not self-assured, independent, and reliant; or able to act without continual direction. The only performance obstacle that all new hires had to overcome was learning to follow. By definition, they only hired those that were independent in thought and action. Being an independent follower was oxymoronic. But it was "follow" in a different sense that they learned.

The company founder was a like-spirited fellow who had somehow gotten through the hiring screen of the first company he joined right out of grad school. Doc (as everyone called him) developed a reputation as a pain in the ass. But he was accepted because of the continuum of contributions that went quickly to the bottom-line. The first few years on the technical career ladder suited both him and the company just fine. He did the work he loved, and management could pigeonhole him as a geek, a good marriage for awhile.

But Doc developed an itch, which rapidly grew into a full blown infection. Doc looked around him and saw great ideas going uncultivated (many his). It was upsetting. He knew that the idea doesn't make money on its own. What he had learned was that if you get a good group of people together, and put them in an environment where most of the walls are torn down, ordinary ideas can blossom and make a lot of money.

So Doc went and made his case about releasing him to pursue some of his ideas on his own. The decision makers recognized a good thing – get rid of a pain and gain a customer because all his ideas would need company products.

Doc resigned and walked out with intellectual property rights in hand. He started his new business in his garage (much to the chagrin of his wife Joyce). At the start, a few good things happened quickly, along with setbacks. Every day was a rollercoaster ride.

Joyce joined him (with baby on her hip). The business progressed and together they transitioned from dead broke to borderline broke in twenty months. Opportunity was now just another employee away, or so it seemed. Now Joyce had a lot of common sense. She knew that Doc couldn't run a business. The monotony of the mundane would kill him. She recognized if the business were going to grow, she'd have to take over the day to day operations, all the while raising children and keeping the family together.

So Joyce took over the operation of the company, including HR. She'd married a maverick. So she figured if one maverick was good for business, a field full would be even better. Joyce also had a sixth sense. She got along well enough with the "tech talk" around the business. But what she was best at understanding was what wasn't said. If you were going to lie to her, you'd better not do it over the phone or face to face. She could read the sound of your voice and your body language perfectly. She was the ideal hiring screen to determine fit. Doc could judge the technical savvy.

And so the company grew - a field full of mavericks functioning within the order imposed by Joyce, the CEO. She liked balancing Freedom and Order. She looked at the people coming in as unbranded and full of potential – and she and the systems she put in place were their guardians.

Joyce was a powerful resource when dealing with the outside world. Doc needed her when talking to suppliers and customers. She often went on business trips at first under her maiden name but later known simply as "the Boss." She used her special gift of always catching a lie. Not that a supplier would ever lie to a customer or vice versa.

If You Are What You Eat, Your Company Is What It Thinks

That's the company Harry hired into. Nobody had titles, "Just creates problems," Joyce often said. Harry flourished as did most that could handle the expanded freedom. People hired in either stayed forever or left in the first few months. Freedom is not a one-way street; it comes with the burden of accountability, and to some the burden was too much.

Order was on an as needed basis when there was a good business reason. Joyce understood how to nurture mavericks, and her rules of order were simple – if you're going to try something that might start a fire that could burn down "the house" you'd better come see her and Doc first. Otherwise, there were no limits on what you could explore or the possibilities you could try to turn into reality. From the outside, it might look like chaos, but there was an order that could only be understood from the inside. It wasn't written; the thinking that managed the order was understood and followed.

Harry was taken aback when he first joined by hearing "Go for it!" As a lifelong maverick, he was accustomed to hearing "No!"

Harry loved the adventure and the turmoil. He loved the uncertainty and the rush of adrenaline you can only find in discovery and breaking new ground. He never liked being pocketed or pigeonholed. He loved the business trail and its mystery as much as the open spaces. And so did all. Nobody was ever branded. The possibilities had no horizon.

Doc's company grew and prospered. And while many studied it, none could come close to emulating it. The invention to market innovation ratio was something all admired. Joyce was the one who created the company's genetic thinking code and set the processes in place to enable all the mavericks. She never said a lot. She just smiled a lot.

Within every organization, there is a continual struggle between Freedom and Order, most often found running out of sight just under the surface and less frequently in open rebellion. Absolute Freedom is Chaos. Absolute Order is Oppression. How this balance is led and managed, channels Corporate Think. Fear is a damper that stifles Freedom – it suppresses creative thinking and is the guardian of "what is" and the status quo.

There are a number of industries that because of "industry regulations" and the fear of consequences of noncompliance result in an isomorphic effect of "customer experience sameness". This isomorphic effect results in "seen one – seen them all" and "what's the difference who I deal with" perception of customers.

More typical are companies in less restrictive environments where the balance of Freedom and Order is under the control of management. The management mindset is the throttle that enables or disables diversity of thinking and divergence from the norm.

Companies can be categorized by their prevailing management style – Bossing – Managing – Leading. Doc and Joyce were leaders where Order was "let us decide if your idea might cause serious harm" to Freedom "go and make a difference." Leading opens the door to what Could Be. Managing closes the door and limits outcomes to what Should Be. Bossing locks the door to What Is.

In Harry's case, following was about embracing the dream, staying focused on it, and understanding the boundaries of order. In the case of a Managed environment, it's about following the SOP. In

If You Are What You Eat, Your Company Is What It Thinks

the case of Bossing, it is about doing what you are told. Each work environment style produces trademark results.

The balance of Freedom and Order is the watchdog of organizational thinking. Bossing results in oppression of thought. But Leading can result in absolute chaos if unbounded. Each company, down to micro-organizations within larger companies, has a framework regulating Freedom and Order. Uncovering it, understanding it, and acting on it is an essential yet frequently overlooked element of "Corporate Think".

If You Are What You Eat, Your Company Is What It Thinks

If You Are What You Eat, Your Company Is What It Thinks

Chapter 8

"RUMORS"

In Aesop's fable, the tortoise beats the hare. Slow and steady wins the race. No matter how many times you read this fable, it comes out the same. The problem is, in the business world there is no finish line. The race is always on. So where does slow and steady get you?

What does that say about Aesop? How do these fables fit the business world? Maybe the "Astronomer" (not paying attention to what's right under your feet); or the "Crow and the Pitcher" (thinking out of the box); or it might be "The Ass, the Fox, and the Lion" (failed alliances - we've all seen that one).

Some scholars claim Aesop was alive and well in the Fifth Century. Others have him as an early version of Mother Goose perpetuated by the likes of Plato. But I'm partial to the story that Aesop did live; that he did write the raft of fables we hang onto to this day. Some have it that Aesop met his end when he annoyed one too many folks and was sentenced to death. He was subsequently executed by being pushed off a cliff. If he had lived he might have written a fable about the fool who kicked the king in the groin, but did not land a fatal blow. The moral of that fable is if you kick someone in the crotch higher up in the corporate pecking order; you better make sure it's fatal.

Regardless, Aesop left us with a deeply ingrained tradition of the plodder a.k.a. the tortoise. My mother would always pull that tale out of her bag of tricks when I began to flinch doing yard work. The tradition of the plodder is part of who we are.

Alroy was a polished plodder. Plodder doesn't mean she was dim-witted. She wasn't. The fact be told; she was way up there on the intelligence scale. She had a finely honed Irish sense of humor which complemented her red hair for which she was named. Alroy is a boy's name, the selection of which her parents never fully explained. So having a sense of humor and a bit of Irish under the surface helped her through grade school. She found it also helped her later in life when she joined the "boys club" of the technology world. Her colleagues' wives had a hard time thinking of their husbands working with a red-haired Irish beauty, so the name Alroy was a good cover – her parents must have seen the future in selecting her name so as not to be artificially discriminated against.

Alroy had to struggle throughout school to keep up her concentration and maintain good grades. Quite frankly, most studies bored her. She was always too smart for whatever course she was taking at the time. She was one of those that when they hit college, went to the bookstore and bought all the books for each class. Then she read them before class started. And that was that. The rest of the semester was drudgery.

While Alroy was getting her Ph.D., in a brand of science that only a few can spell much less pronounce, she had struggled with the mandatory classes. But Aesop's fable, so well engrained by her Mom, sustained her.

Companies like Toyota have been built on a foundation of slow and steady. Decisions are reached slowly. But because of the system of engagement and thoroughly considering not only the problem but solutions, implementation is fast. There is nothing wrong with "plodding" organizational thought processes, as long as there are decisions and slow and steady does not become a dodge to avoid a decision and the reason for the cliché – paralysis by analysis. Plodding means to work slowly but steadily, especially on something uninteresting or laborious, and there is plenty of that in the world of business.

After graduation she was confronted with, as most newly hired are, mundane and uninteresting tasks. She had hired into a company that was trumpeted as the market leader; an innovator of technology. She didn't get the purpose behind taking someone such as herself and immersing her in trivial pursuit. But she accepted it and very soon her boss recognized she was exceptionally good at accomplishing the mundane at the same time some of her peers not only struggled but were complaining covertly and overtly.

Alroy's boss and mentor knew she was not enamored by the assignments and told her, "Be patient. Good things will come. Just stick with it." The "voice of her mother" which she thought she had finally escaped. After a few months, her boss decided to ratchet it up and turned her loose on a couple of "Mission Impossible" tasks. These were problems that had nagged the company for ages, and the organization had built in "workarounds" to cope with them. They had frustrated the chrome off many of the erstwhile stars that had preceded her. But to the astonishment of her boss Alroy figured them out.

Max (the newly hired CEO) believed that being assigned to strategic tasks wasn't an entitlement – it had to be earned. It was one of those unwritten rules he held too tightly to the vest, so tight that no one understood it. While it should have been obvious, there were "tenure" and "projecting upwards" advancement traditions left over from the preceding CEO.

So when Alroy leapfrogged into the "strategic technical circle" there was a lot of background chatter about a hot babe getting to the top. She wasn't seen by her peers as a high flier. She kept low-key, and her accomplishments had stayed mostly under the organization's radar.

Max was a flamboyant type. Outgoing and no matter who he talked to, they always walked away feeling good. He had that way about him. Few remembered what he said, but they all remembered how they felt after conversing with him. Getting close to Max was something everyone sought. And Max made it easy spending 80% of his time away from his desk, on the road and out with the organization. Now Max was a good listener, a fundamental part of his leadership persona. But you can't hear what isn't spoken. Innuendo is a subtle sort of thing – the between the lines that sometimes becomes more important than what is on the lines. Say what you mean and mean what you say, being direct, is not a natural thing beyond childhood. So nobody directly challenged Max on Alroy's rapid ascension. Nobody ever asked why, they "just knew."

Alroy had learned being good looking, smart, and athletic wasn't the best thing if you wanted to be popular in high school. Boys were afraid of you and girls resented you. Alroy got wind of the rumbling and took it in stride, same-old-same-old. Alroy was assigned to a team responding to a problem marketing saw coming up over the horizon. When the team was chartered Max took a personal hand in picking who would be on it and Alroy was an easy pick in his mind but at the same time her selection fueled the innuendo mill.

The "legend" of Alroy's advancement preceded her into the team of good 'ol boys that had been assembled. So Alroy was assigned a role on the team that was once again the mundane. But, as they say, the devil is in the detail, and Alroy's plodding dug out the needed kernels of truth that became the springboard for a breakthrough. The team was surprised with what Alroy synthesized from picking through the "garbage detail" she had been given. But technology is technology and it levels the playing field. So within the team Alroy came into her own and was recognized for who she was and what she could contribute.

But outside the team, the legend of Alroy's vertical rise via "horizontal positioning" was becoming even more solidified. Unwittingly Max had created a new story. Jeanne was Max' executive assistant – an extremely important and powerful well-compensated position. The fact that she had an MBA was not well known. One of Jeanne's skills was putting her ear to the rail and listening for oncoming trains. She heard the Alroy train building up steam. When Max touched base, Jeanne informed him he had a mess (being direct was one of Jeanne's core skills).

Undoing innuendo and rumors after they get dug in is difficult. But with Max's style it didn't take too long for him to fix it by personally carrying the message of the new values by which he wanted to reshape the organization.

Plodding is an attribute, not a "classification." Being an attractive female doesn't classify a person either.

If You Are What You Eat, Your Company Is What It Thinks

Stories are the inertial thinking system of an organization. Intended or unintended they exist. They have to be recognized and understood. Rumors are a mainstay in all organizations, a cry for understanding. Rumors, like the one initially built around Alroy, are a cancer that eats away at an organization.

Building the right stories fuels, energizes, and sustains organizations and keeps Corporate Think centered and on track. Rumors side track and sometimes derail an effort if left unbridled.

If You Are What You Eat, Your Company Is What It Thinks

Chapter 9

"SOUNDERS"

A sounder is a herd of wild pigs. Typical are groups of 20 including mothers and their offspring. The male boars don't hangout except during the mating season – typical male chauvinist pigs. In New Zealand wild pigs are referred to as "Captain Cookers" after, of course, Captain Cook, who first released pigs carried aboard the Endeavor ca. 1769. Regardless of continent or location if you stumble onto one in the wild they can give you quite a start. They're omnivores and are most active at night. And contrary to the popular expression, pigs don't sweat. That expression has its roots in the foundry.

The idea of small teams had always intrigued Sam. The ad hoc teams he had been a part of provided his most enjoyable work memories from before he quit and started his own company. He always kept those experiences in the back of his mind. As time went on he developed a mental picture of himself at the hub of a wheel with spokes running out to small teams.

In the years that had passed since startup, Sam felt a growing sense of losing ground and falling behind. It felt like being in a dream where you are running faster and faster but not going anywhere. The more successful the company became, the less able they were to do what had made them successful. His company was becoming lethargic. It was on a plateau. It seemed like collectively they had fallen off the horse that had gotten them there and worse yet, they were eating it for breakfast, lunch, and dinner – and this wasn't France.

One Saturday morning it hit him. Now was the time to reshape the company. The more he thought about the possibility, the more gripping it became. When he had formed the company, they were a sounder of 'Captain Cookers' (Sam always liked that analogy) out in the bush in unexplored lands. Of course, he was the alpha male boar. Somebody had to be.

"Perfect," Sam thought. "It's time to get back to our roots. I can keep my hand on the pulse, my ear to the ground, and things will start moving again like they used to." As he visualized how all this would come together, he saw the prospect of no longer requiring the logjam of staff between himself and the action. "I can put these experienced resources to work attacking the growing 'want-to-do' list. We've become so bound up handling the 'need to do' it's dragging us down."

By Sunday night Sam had mapped it out, what it would look and feel like when the company got there. It was exhilarating. Next step was to educate his staff and get them working with him on implementing it.

Monday morning Sam got his senior staff together and laid out his "wheel vision". There were very few questions. Sam interpreted that as buy-in. At the end of the meeting Sam said, "We need to start working back from that future and decide what our next steps are. There will be obstacles, but it's time we move on."

If You Are What You Eat, Your Company Is What It Thinks

On Wednesday, Wayne, the SVP of Operations, came into Sam's office and closed the door. Sam thought "This must be serious. We never close doors around here. I don't know why we paid for them when we built this place." Sam was all ears. Wayne spoke, "This won't work. I've been thinking about it, and it just won't work." Wayne had not been part of the startup team and had been brought in when Sam realized no one in the original group knew much about day to day operations or for that matter cared.

Wayne explained how Sam's vision of everyone in the company being "one spoke away" from Sam was ludicrous. Wayne went on, "I've been in operations my whole career. I've seen about everything from big play touchdowns to fumbles on the one yard line with less than a minute to play and victory in sight (Wayne was a big ACC football fan). What you're proposing is an absolute disaster. I cannot be a part of it. You have to choose – back away from this ridiculousness – or me."

Now Sam didn't get to where he was by being indecisive. So he looked Wayne in the eye and said, "I appreciate you being direct with me. It was one of the reasons I hired you. And I agree you can't be a part of something you don't believe in. So I'm going to give you a one-year severance in salary, and benefits coverage until you get your feet back on the ground. You can count on me as your first and best reference. I have no reservations about giving you a glowing endorsement. You were the perfect fit for where we were. I'm sorry you don't see yourself in our future."

And that was that. However, Wayne's departure was like kicking a hornets' nest. The rumor mill became so loud it was deafening. Wayne's departure was quickly becoming a self-fulfilling prophecy if Sam didn't do something.

If You Are What You Eat, Your Company Is What It Thinks

Sam was a good student. He had read over and over again about CEO's who were brought in to turn around companies, and then had fallen flat on their faces. He resolved he wasn't going to be the next business news headline of the once successful and now failed CEO. Wayne had been loyal, but he could see the "I told you so" business news quotes coming, and takeover vultures soaring above dropping lowball offers until the customers and people lost faith and started going elsewhere.

Sam had more than a flicker of doubt. The company was reverberating within hours of Wayne's departure. He knew in his gut that moving ahead reshaping how the company came together and did its work was the right thing to do, but still . . .what if his company had been stocked with "Wayne's" as it grew? "Would the resistance be too much to overcome?" he pondered.

That first night after Wayne's departure was more than just fitful. Sam's wife Judy told him he just couldn't go off half-cocked when people are involved and expect anything different. "You're just too comfortable with chasing technology. People aren't numbers in a spreadsheet. They see Wayne's leaving and now are wondering what is going to happen to them. You need to fix this!" Truer words were never spoken - spouses have a knack for that.

Sam spent the rest of a sleepless night considering the options. Maybe bring in a consulting firm and put on a Kaizen event targeting our management system – but that seemed like a waste of time. Offhand he didn't know of any firms dealing with anything other than operations. He'd been through a Kaizen event in his previous corporate life. His and his colleagues' perception back then was that it was disingenuous – "Where's management!" Plus it would take too long to organize and implement. He had to act.

If You Are What You Eat, Your Company Is What It Thinks

But what to do? Maybe with his staff, craft a memo to the organization? Their past efforts at this had been memos coming out looking more like a "camel" than the "thoroughbred race horse" they were intended to be. Send HR communications teams out? But did HR really get it? His whole vision of a company of sounders was looking more and more like him being a pig tied onto a rotisserie over a fire pit.

Sam reckoned that the only way to get this done lay in his hands and his hands alone. So the next day, he cleared his calendar for the next two months. A real mess for his executive assistant to straighten out – but Joan was that good. He then told his staff what he was up to. A lot of jaws dropped, so Sam said, "You have the bridge. I'm redundant right now. We need to get on with this. I started it, and I need to finish it."

For the next two months Sam spent every working minute talking and personally teaching every person in the company what he meant; what needed to happen; and how to go about doing it. Chief Educator and Facilitator was not what Sam had in mind when he started this, but it became readily apparent after a few weeks, that this is what he needed to do.

Some greeted his vision with open arms; some did not; and some took a wait and see. "This is going to take longer than I thought" Sam mused. What he was proposing meant there would be a lot of roles eliminated and people redeployed. And it was becoming crystal clear that the first job to go was the role that he had grown into before he started all this. Sam thought, "I was stupid to think that the organization was the one to change and not me too." So Sam stuck with it. Two months turned out to be only the first of many mile markers.

If You Are What You Eat, Your Company Is What It Thinks

In three months, Sam could feel the organization creaking and groaning trying to change course with a sluggish helm. In five months, he could see the new course he had laid out taking shape. In nine months he could feel the organization picking up speed as most of the people had gotten off the sidelines and jumped in, from manufacturing to R&D to sales. People were getting on board.

At the end of the first year, Sam pondered what his next steps should be. Chief Educator and Facilitator was not a role he had intended to be in when he started the company. But it seemed to be working. The "want-to-do" list had been coming down, but now for every two items that came off the list another popped up like a summer thunderstorm. And that was all good. Some of the items that had come off the list were already impacting the bottom-line. It was quickly discovered that others should have never been on the list in the first place. But the fact that they were taken up, instead of just sitting there on the list, was a shot in the arm for morale.

Sam reread and researched again all the corporate miscues he had collected. The common thread was CEO's who thought that standing on the bully pulpit was good enough. So Sam continued on with his newly found role of Chief Educator and Facilitator traveling through the company engaging with everyone, and only getting directly involved with below-the-waterline corporate decisions. He found as time passed that he and the organization were better able to deal with these below-the-waterline issues than they ever had been. As the layers of management and supervision were peeled away, and experienced people redeployed, the organization became not only self-sustaining but the speed and energy made a step change as they took hold.

If You Are What You Eat, Your Company Is What It Thinks

    The "voice" of a leader is neither hands-off, nor is it handed off. Corporate Think is a cause and effect result of what people can see and experience as leaders directly train and then teach through their repetitive actions. It requires a clear head, concentration, and follow-through. In the best of circumstances, a leader's actions that are "out of bounds" will be quickly challenged. A leader then has to be even quicker at saying they messed up; and "thank you!" Admitting you're wrong is not a sign of weakness. Fact be told, half the time you are wrong, and the other half is up for grabs.

If You Are What You Eat, Your Company Is What It Thinks

Chapter 10

"FLOCK BIRDS"

At some point, we've all seen and marveled at the seemingly endless river of migrating birds that extend over the horizon in a continuous flow effortlessly curving and bending, changing direction without any apparent signal.

Alice had completed her undergrad in engineering at a land-grant university and followed that with an Ivy League MBA. She had great job offers on graduating, and was able to be very selective. She loved the technology at the company she joined. She could see it evolving and solving more and more consumer problems that once were stipulated by markets and customers as unsolvable.

Alice progressed rapidly, sometimes as window dressing and for diversity stats. But "Oh well" she ruminated, "Ride the wave while it is there." But increasingly her advancement was for merit and less and less for "the numbers." Alice had married and experienced her childrearing responsibilities as increasingly an object lesson in management.

By the time empty nest had arrived, Alice was positioned and ready for senior management – just not with the company where she started. The BOD still had a chauvinistic management model in their collective head. They saw diversity as an end not a means. Alice had reached the end of the line aka the "glass ceiling." She loved the company. They had been great with family support policies and practices. A rarity she knew. But when an inquiry came from a company in another noncompeting industry she felt it was time.

Alice asked her husband Joe, who she had met in engineering school, what he thought. Joe had quickly abandoned a corporate career and started a shop maintaining and repairing high-end performance import cars, his true passion. People came from miles around to have his shop take care of their "toys."

Joe said, "Look. You'll always regret it if you don't give it a go. See where it leads."

Alice said, "We'll have to move. What about the shop?"

"We can keep this shop and I'll open a satellite one. I've got staff in place to handle the day-to-day, and the area surrounding your new company's corporate offices is rich with high-end toys. They even have Ferrari and Maserati dealerships there so I'll have an ample supply of technicians ready to make the jump to my business model which is a whole lot more generous than being attached to a dealership."

So the offer came through, and Alice moved into the CEO spot. Joe opened his satellite repair shop with near immediate success. Reputation carries long distances in specialized market segments. You don't spend megabucks on toys without getting into the enthusiast's network, and Joe's brand was well known in the network.

Alice launched her new career with a two-week meet-and-greet tour. When she got back home she told Joe, "The Company sounds like a flock of Mockingbirds with the racket of their multiple personality disorder singing."

Joe laughed. They had a mockingbird in their backyard who started the endless chant of every birdcall it had ever heard somewhere around 4 a.m. on the roof above their bedroom. They'd somehow had missed that pleasure at their last house.

Alice said, "It was hard to stay focused and listen after the first few days of this babble. I've come back totally unclear with what this company thinks it is supposed to be doing. It is a bigger mess than what I was led to believe by the Board." She knew from her engineering background that leading was a process just like manufacturing or order entry and fulfillment. Creating visions was only a step in the process, and it looked like the previous leadership had spewed out lots of those.

The following Monday she sat down with her executive assistant Ginger. Alice spoke, "We have to get to know each other, but how comfortable are you if I asked you a few questions about my predecessor?"

Ginger replied, "If I don't answer the question, it won't be because I didn't hear you."

So Alice related her experiences of the last two weeks.

Ginger thought for a bit and then said, "Big Jim was a big idea kind of manager. That would explain what you heard. Look, the word on you is that you are a good listener. You asked good questions, and people appreciated that you had heard them. Don't get me wrong. Everybody liked Big Jim. But the story line on him was he would throw bread pieces on the water and didn't wait to see who came after them. It was onto the next big idea. I'm sorry to see Jim leave the way he did, but it was getting crazy."

With that, Alice sat down and started sketching out a leadership process (engineers like to sketch). She knew that there were only three levels of activity in leading – Choosing, Planning and Doing. And within each level there were three additive sub-activities Target, Align, and Implement. Starting to overlay what she had heard, Big Jim and the senior leaders had never gotten past Choosing (and they chose about everything) and the organization went right to implementing. It explained how a common theme was a lack of resources and complaints about competing agendas.

"Hmmm," Alice pondered. "Had the senior management team not recognized what was happening? Or had they set Big Jim up for a belly flop on the concrete floor when he dove off the stage into the "mosh pit" expecting to be caught?" Turning back to Ginger, Alice said, "I have a theory. Big Jim was set up to fail by his staff. And you would say?"

Ginger hesitated; this was getting into uncomfortable territory. Ginger finally spoke, "You're on the right trail. And so you know, the senior staff is very comfortable with "THEIR WAY" and they see you as a threat to that. Going out into the organization without being under their direct control was just not in their playbook."

"Enough said" Alice replied.

At home that night over a late dinner with Joe she told him about what she had found. "Don't worry," Joe said with a grin "You can always come to work at the shop." After a not-so-funny but I forgive you stare, Joe said "You know what to do. Just do it."

Early the next morning Alice called the Board Chair and said she wanted to talk to the full BOD. The Board Chair replied, "I was hoping for this call when we hired you. And so was the rest of the board. We can meet the day after tomorrow." "Darn," Alice thought to herself after hanging up. "What did the Chairman mean by that? Well, maybe putting on a pair of coveralls and going to work at the shop wasn't such a bad option."

With Ginger's help, Alice put a presentation together without any input from the rest of her staff. Ginger said, "You're pissing off your staff. Talking to the board without their input is bad enough – but them not knowing what you're going to say is way worse."

Alice replied, "Be sure to tell me if you get any ugly threats or innuendoes. I will put an end to that in a way that will make everyone sit up straight in their chairs."

Ginger said, "None yet that I can't handle."

When Alice got to the Board meeting she explained what she had found and used her sketch (cleaned up by Ginger) and what she planned to do ending with "I need your full support without equivocation." After a silent pause, one clap led to another and another with each Board member chiming in their support.

And so the journey began, first with Senior Staff. One of whom went directly from the introductory meeting and made a call to a buddy board member with his complaint. The Board member said, "I'll call Alice and tell her you have resigned effective immediately. I'll get your package together. Let's get out trout fishing at the end of the month. The weather should be great."

If You Are What You Eat, Your Company Is What It Thinks

"It's so nice to have a Board who speaks with its actions," Alice thought. She now had her senior management's full attention. Business as usual was history. "THEIR WAY" was relegated to a scrapbook. And so it went.

Corporate Think is so embedded it takes "fracking" to break up entrenched rituals and processes. This ingrained thinking devours any initiative or change it confronts. This rooted thinking is the foundation that supports "wait and see." It is the flow that effortlessly keeps the organization curving and bending, changing direction without any apparent signal. Changing the flow of thought isn't easy, but once in place it is effortless like a flock of birds moving in a new direction.

Before strategies and tactics comes organizational thinking. Getting this order reversed always results in stalled initiatives no matter how good they might be.

Chapter 11

"BE GOOD OR BE GOOD AT IT"

Look at any situation where action is required then brainstorm all the possible responses. If you stack them all up, you will have a pretty tall tower. When you take off the "horse blinkers" the possibilities and nuances for action are almost limitless.

If you then sort through them and put the unquestionably illegal possibilities at the base with the most illegal as the foundation and then build the stack up using paired order ranking you get to a point in the stack that attorneys refer to as the "grey area." That line is an inflection point transitioning from "being good at it" to "being good."

Continuing on with the pairing process, the next possible actions, just above the grey area, are those that would not pass the "smell test" – legal but by most all standards unethical. Continue stacking until you reach the top where the actions would be hailed as virtuous and setting the watermark of ethical behavior.

Bill had worked hard to keep his grades above 3.8 – the entry level GPA for many companies. So when he landed a job with a "named company" it was one of the best days of his life. He looked at the future and envisioned a pathway best described as the "yellow brick road."

Bill got the offer in February. When he got the call, his first thought was to find Ann (his college sweetheart) and celebrate. With graduation now in sight, their relationship was being confronted with a dilemma. The job was on the other coast far from Ann's family and friends. Bill's thumb hung above the speed dial number. The decision was huge. Does their relationship progress or will this job end it? Whose career would be the lead and whose would follow? Marriage? What about the college loans?

This job offer was a whole lot more than just a job. This decision was a life event. While it opened doors, it closed just as many. Bill and Ann sorted it all out, were married a week after graduation, and set off for the opposite coast in a 12-year old compact car with their worldly possessions either crammed inside or strapped on the roof. Their honeymoon was the cross-country drive. They were both realists – broke is broke; and they were broke plus somebody had to get to work and crank up the money machine, or they'd be back living with their parents – not cool.

The company had given them a relocation package. They had rented a nice garden apartment in a great location which was awaiting their arrival, albeit totally devoid of furnishings. Their camping air mattress upgraded with a Memory Foam® wedding gift topper would work just fine. The company HR department had networked around and had lined up several interviews for Ann. How good was that!

Ann and Bill settled in. Within two months, Ann had landed a great job to launch her career and better yet they had moved off the floor and into a real bed. Their "train" was out of the station and moving down the tracks.

If You Are What You Eat, Your Company Is What It Thinks

Bill quickly assimilated into the company, and within four months was a "member of the team". After two years on the job, Bill was given a promotion and the additional responsibility of membership to the Rapid Response Team (RRT). The team handled everything from onerous customer complaints to questions that made their way to the CEO's attention.

It was quite an honor. Most of the other RRT team members had passed the 25-year service mark. Bill held them in awe. The RRT was revered as the corporate brain trust, and he had just been made part of it.

Ann and Bill celebrated and decided it was time to move out of the apartment and find a house.

In the next year, the RRT was only called on once, and it had to do with writing a press release.

Life was good!

It was on a Saturday morning when Bill got the call to come in ASAP. The RRT had been activated for a second time. There had been a failure in an infant car seat to which they supplied parts.

It was 10 a.m. when the team got together and 11:30 p.m. that night by the time they had completed a Fault Tree Analysis (FTA). They discovered that the redesigned more cost effective part that had been rolled out seven months ago by a continuous improvement team had a design flaw. The FTA had zeroed in on a stress riser that when exposed to forces present in certain kinds of crashes would cause the infant seat to fail catastrophically. With the specificity of the crash details and using the USDOT database one could expect a failure once every 10,860,000 hours accumulated car seat highway exposure. With

125,000 of these specific car seats in use and using an average of 60 hours per year travel time, they could expect on average one possible fatal infant accident every two years.

The CEO wanted a meeting at 5 a.m. Sunday morning. Bill was "elected" to put together a presentation, and lead the meeting. He was barely able to finish up, get home, shower, change clothes and get back in time. Ann asked what the heck was going on. Bill told her to go back to sleep, and he'd tell her later.

Bill's presentation went well with only questions for clarity that he answered easily and amplified by other team members when there were follow-up questions. By 6:30 a.m. the meeting was over, and Bill was on his way home.

Ann was up when he got home, and he filled her in. Ann said, "Good Lord! This is awful!" Bill said that the team had recommended a recall even though a company tech would have to disassemble and retrofit each infant seat. You couldn't just send a part and expect the infant seat owners to get it right. It was going to be an expensive proposition.

When Bill got in Monday morning Jim, the RRT leader, was sitting at Bill's desk. Jim had gotten the word that legal wanted all the hardcopies of the presentation and any notes and charts from the team meeting. They also wanted any emails to be deleted from personal computers as well as any documents. Jim was there to ensure it happened. IT had already wiped the email server. RRT's analysis and all traces of the meeting were to vanish.

Bill was shocked. He admired Jim and asked what the heck was going on. Jim said, "Look kid. You're good. There isn't going to be a recall. It's time to stand up and salute. Do you get what I'm saying? This is not my decision. This is why senior management gets paid the big bucks to make the call."

Jim did what was requested. He felt queasy the rest of the day and couldn't concentrate. The people around him didn't even know he'd spent the weekend at work, and he had been told not to discuss it. When he got home that night, Ann asked excitedly how it went. Jim told her and added emphatically that he had thought about this all day, and resigning was something he was thinking about. To which Ann replied with a tear running down her cheek – "I'm pregnant." And such is life.

The undercurrents of "a wink and a nod"; "nod and salute"; and "don't ask don't tell" are often difficult to detect. But when they happen, they work their way into the fabric of company thinking. This demonstrated attitude permeates a company, expanding into ever smaller and smaller decisions with ever increasing impact. Push the limits; "Be good at it" becomes the emblem of success.

Leading is taking a stand. Saying what you mean and demonstrating it. Pulling back from the "line in the sand," aka "flinching," is a very loud leadership voice. Albeit a whisper – but if you want someone to hear something, whisper. Flinching is always perceived, translated and travels well beyond the initial event.

To flinch or not to flinch – that is the question. Does a company really mean what it says; can it be trusted? A leader's actions define and continually redefine the lines of behavior and acceptability in a company. Leadership actions are the guardians and perpetuators of Corporate Think and resulting conduct.

For ethical businesses, it isn't a choice to cross the line into criminal behavior; and "being good at it" is never in the mix.

If You Are What You Eat, Your Company Is What It Thinks

If You Are What You Eat, Your Company Is What It Thinks

Chapter 12

"PINNIPEDS"

Pinniped in Latin means "feather or fin foot." The term is used by the scientific community in reference to seals, sea lions, and walruses. These mammals are awkward on land but powerful and graceful in the water.

Everyone enjoys watching California sea lions at the zoo or lounging around in harbors. Not so cool is taking the family boat out in the bay fishing and watching "cute" sea lions crawl up on your boat's swim platform. Sea lions have a nasty set of teeth, and males, at 600+ pounds each, don't just shoo away. They have been known to swamp boats. If you poke at them and they feel threatened they roar. You have to wonder whether Katy Perry's "Roar" wasn't inspired by sea lions.

Not so well known is their ability to communicate. The calliope of barks, grunts, growls, and trumpets are all part of the process. When you're standing there watching them you begin to wonder "What are they saying about us?" or "Why did they just laugh?" About the same feeling you get in a restaurant where the wait staff is talking in a language not your mother tongue.

Bill started his professional life in a company where "dedication" translated as "long hours." After five years, he had yet to

If You Are What You Eat, Your Company Is What It Thinks

meet a member of senior management. Although they were adored and some might say worshiped, nobody ever saw them except on the stage at company galas and in videocasts. He was feeling totally burned out. There was a fairly high rate of turnover, but this was the bang-bang world of high tech. There were always people leaving, but there was also a line waiting to come onboard. He had ideas but they never went anywhere. He felt like he was shouting into a vacuum chamber.

One Saturday morning he met up with Fred, his old college roommate, who was now a marine biologist. They went for a run along the harbor walk. Afterward they got a cappuccino from one of the ubiquitous coffee shops and sat on a bench overlooking the harbor.

Sitting there you couldn't ignore the noise coming from the congregated sea lions. So Bill asked Fred about them. Fred replied that he wasn't really into sea mammals but beyond their communicating, they were really intelligent and could be trained. The US Navy has a program called The Navy Marine Mammal Program (NMMP) and they train sea lions for different tasks. They could dive over 500 feet, stay under water for a half hour, and hit 25 MPH under water when they wanted. They were very social. That's why they are all clumped together instead of spread out. They even worked together on occasions as a team.

When Bill asked if he could tell what they were saying, Fred replied that nobody he knew of had actually broken the code yet. Bill thought about the conversation for weeks afterwards. With all that chaotic noise, sea lions could still hear each other and understand. Swift and agile, ferocious yet friendly, quick to learn, open and communicating – it sure sounded like a recipe for a company that would be fun to work for.

If You Are What You Eat, Your Company Is What It Thinks

Several weeks later Bill and a friend John got together at a nearby microbrewery and were watching the crowd while sipping "this week's" brew special. They were particularly paying attention to the women who were constantly playing with their smartphones. Bill started thinking, "Wouldn't it be great, with all the noise and the crowd in here, if you could get a message over to that brunette in the corner on her smartphone without having her in your contacts?" Bill spouted out the idea to John more as a joke. They started batting the idea around and the more they talked the more excited they got – it was moving from the ridiculous toward the real.

Bill thought to himself, "I could really get into this!" The "burned out" cloud hovering over him seemed to be lifting, or maybe it was the brew. Regardless, Bill thought further. If he went to the company where he worked and suggested it, he knew the answer "Cool idea but this isn't really in our wheelhouse." And the cloud started coming back.

"How about we run with this?" he said

John replied, "Okay. Let's get together next Saturday after the brew stops talking and see if there really is something there."

For the next three months John and Bill met every Saturday at John's apartment, 8 to 8. The idea kept evolving and building, and every Saturday was a renewal to some degree. The week long break gave them a fresh set of eyes each Saturday morning. They wrote code, tried different things, and continued to develop a technology solution that went beyond the typical dating site thing, and tackled the problem of how do you introduce yourself to someone you see without being a creep or a predator. How do you connect with someone vanishing in a crowd you would like to meet without shouting some lame pickup line? How do women meet men – it wasn't just a guy problem – without coming across as a stalker or worse.

They got to a point in their product development where they needed to decide – are we all in or not – scary. This had been a fun exercise, but now they were looking at jumping into an abyss that would be a life changing experience one way or the other. They decided to go for it, sucked it up, quit their jobs, moved into an apartment together and went to work 24/7. Having no income was frightening. Their horizon was as far as their checking account balance and their credit card limits.

Things moved quickly for them and within a year from financing to launch they had formed a business, employed five people, and were seeing a sustained flow of income. By leveraging social media tools they were quickly moving from local to regional to national, and global seemed to be within reach. This all meant "more". And so they grew.

One Saturday Bill had a 'significant emotional event'. He was sitting at the harbor sipping cappuccino with his marine biologist friend Fred after a run. A passing runner in a colorful body suit came up and jogging in place said, "Hi Bill. The telecast Friday was great!" She said "See you" and quickly disappeared from sight.

Fred asked, "Who was that?"

Bill's only response was, "I have no idea."

Bill felt his gut tighten. They now employed over 1,200 people. "Dang," he thought "I've created the company I fled from!"

With a crushing sense of guilt and remorse Bill went to the office Sunday night and started putting his thoughts up on a glass display board they used to deal with complex issues. He placed himself in the center. Surrounding him was a galaxy of points representing each employee. The issue was how was he connected?

On Monday he got together with John in front of the board.

John said, "Okay, what am I looking at?"

Bill replied, "Us. We're losing it. We created the same disconnected mess we both broke away from."

Silence.

John spoke up next. "Are you sure we have the problem. Maybe people don't feel that way."

Silence.

Then John said, "Am I in denial?"

Bill responded, "We need to be a company of pinnipeds."

Silence.

John finally spoke, "What's a pinniped?"

Bill retold his epiphany watching the sea lions. "We were that when we started and now it's gone. We've both become just fog horns. As we grew we took our eye off what made us different. Success is doing us in. We didn't deal with it." And so the journey back began. They were a company who was created to solve a communication problem. The challenge Bill said was "How do you go about building an individual relationship with over a thousand people and growing?"

Bill and John had HR randomly pick 70 people from all levels of the organization and have them assemble the following Monday. A lot of logistics, but it got done. Calling the meeting was a loud bell that reverberated throughout the organization, getting everyone's attention. The invitation was not specific. It only said "We need your help dealing with a problem." It set off the rumor mill. The organization had been destabilized. People were talking about it.

Showtime – time to start restabilizing. At 7:30 a.m. on the first day of the 3-day meeting Bill and John stood up in front of those assembled and said, "We don't really know you. A few of you we recognize by sight only; others we know from having worked with you before. A couple of you were here at the beginning. But for most of you we have no clue and we deeply regret that."

"We have come together to design a solution to this problem – How do we create an organization where everyone, no matter who they are or where they are, can build a relationship with all the other people in the company? And it starts with John and me."

Bill didn't know where the expression "deafening silence" came from but this sure was it. After a pause that felt more like a day, John asked, "Are there any questions?"

A hand went up and a voice spoke, "How were we picked?" Bill responded, "It was totally random. You are the 70 balls in a twelve hundred ball lottery drawing. You are the winners. This is a critical task. Your talent in developing the answer and rolling it out will shape who we are for decades to come."

If You Are What You Eat, Your Company Is What It Thinks

The deafening silence was breaking up now with the sound of murmuring. Facts were that most of these people didn't know who each other were either.

Bill spoke up, "We're going to do this together, where everyone's voice is heard and their ideas accounted for. It's important. I see us at the brink of lapsing into a rigid, subdued, impersonal organization that is slow to learn and compelling to leave. One might say unfriendly and uncaring about one another. Quite frankly I think we are there and it is my mistake to have let this happen."

"We all have created our own private space, never venturing out and quick to defend it when we feel someone overstepping. We've stopped learning. The root of it is we've stopped communicating."

"When John and I started this company we were in a wide open loft with no walls or cubicles. Everyone could see each other and hear one another. Communicating started with 'Hey Jim. . .' Discussions were spontaneous and constant. Collaboration was easy. Growth has been our friend. But it is going to be our undoing if we don't fix it."

"We are going to break up into ten, seven-person teams. Each team will pick a leader and someone who will be your 'voice' when we get back together. HR is providing you a meeting facilitator and a meeting process to get you going."

As the first day progressed, the murmur moved to a rumble and by the time dinner was ordered in, it was a roar. Teams kept working into the night. The problem was clearly articulated with embarrassing facts that verified Bill's feelings. At the start of the second day, additional people were called in because the teams had found missing skills and knowhow needed to complete the task.

If You Are What You Eat, Your Company Is What It Thinks

By midday on the third day the solution was in hand. A virtual realm had been created where every member of the company had their own avatar (it must have their face and a name tag but the rest was up to a person's imagination) where each could roam through the company and visit anywhere at any time. They could jump on problems or ask for help or just check things out.

The rollout started on Monday, and within a week all 1,200 employees were up and running. By the end of the first month things were happening. The organization had moved from becalmed to full throttle. People were getting to know one another. All were genuinely impressed with each other, and how they could help one another. Seemingly complex technical challenges to meet customers evolving wants were being solved by simple solutions coming from the most unlikely places.

As for Bill, his avatar was a sea lion. The corporate environment he set out to create was coming to life.

Corporate Think can easily morph without notice. It can get caught in a slipstream or riptide, and what once was the norm is no more, dramatically changing the company. During times of transition Corporate Think is most at risk; and without direct stewardship it will go adrift. Whether the transition is brought on by growth or market retrenchment or changing compliance requirements, the risk has to be acknowledged and managed.

Chapter 13

"TOTEMS"

If you want to gain an insight into how a company thinks, pay attention to what's on the walls. From the reception lobbies to mahogany row, the walls tell a story.

Some Native American tribes use carvings called totems to symbolize things of importance using animals or plants to represent them. Their belief is that there are different animals acting as guides that accompany a person through life's journey. They will come in and out of one's life depending on circumstances and the challenges one faces. These animal guides offer power and wisdom.

Companies have an analogous practice. Placed on corporate walls are their totems that guide corporate thinking pointing toward what is important. The emblems that make it to the walls are management's voice elevating to prominence what matters.

Take the Madagascar Nuts & Bolts company, a supplier to a wide range of industries, markets, and applications. The elevator lobby has ancient artifacts on display including vases dating back to the Ming Dynasty. The hallway to the executive suites is covered with collector artworks. The C-suite conference room walls are plastered with portraits of executives who had once carried the company scepter. All that is missing are votive candles.

If You Are What You Eat, Your Company Is What It Thinks

Across town is the headquarters of Weselton, a fast food company. The lobby is filled with posters of the smiling faces of uniformed Weselton teams engaging customers and in community events. The hallway to the executive suite is decorated with framed pictures of news clippings recognizing local Weselton restaurant employees for their community involvement and service. The C-suite conference room walls are covered with posters of employee task teams gathered to celebrate a success.

Around the corner from Weselton is Agrabah's headquarters. From the front door to the C-suite is a showroom for Offices-R-Us, generic stuff devoid of any message, which then opens the door to questioning the message of no message.

On the outskirts of town is the Middleton Inc. plant site. Middleton is a major local employer. One of its first manufacturing facilities was built here shortly after its founding. No matter what corner you turn, or where your eyes wander, there are messages of personal safety and up to date scoreboards as a constant reminder.

Down the interstate is the corporate headquarters of Thunder Clap, LLC. Thunder Clap is a major global supplier of parts and subassemblies to the automotive industry. Everywhere you look there are manufactured parts on display. Shiny inanimate objects abound.

What hangs on the walls and hallways resonate the message of the company thinking through its totems. What's there is the focal point of Corporate Think. What's not there carries a similar weighting to what is there.

Personal workspace is not exempt. Every company has policies that set boundaries on what can be hung or posted from both a legal perspective as well as appropriateness. What hangs on the walls of every individual's space are the totems of who they are. From locker doors to meeting rooms, walls echo thinking.

Not paying attention to the walls of offices and sites is a serious leadership misstep. How corporate totems get to the walls and how the people are engaged in getting the totems there is equally important.

What's on your walls?

If You Are What You Eat, Your Company Is What It Thinks

Chapter 14

"IT APPEARS MY HYPOCRISY KNOWS NO BOUNDS"

This is a memorable line from the 1993 movie "Tombstone" character Doc Holliday. Hypocrisy and its stepchild "spin" have become so ingrained that we no longer cringe when we hear it. Spin rooms are now SOP for political debates.

Alice had been into student government and activism, so making the jump to a political campaign after graduation was a dream come true. Alice quickly progressed from a volunteer envelope stuffer to a full-time staffer. The pay was miniscule, but the action and excitement were addictive. Exhausted yes – lack of energy no. Being an indispensable player in the campaign was like an IV drip of Red Bull®. The campaign events, the meet and greets, the photo ops were all clicking. It was a tough campaign but winning was within reach.

Election Day was eleven days off when Ben, the Chief of Staff, stopped her in the parking lot. Ben said, "We need to get into the blogosphere with what I'm going to tell you and get a hashtag campaign going." He went on detailing the messaging that he wanted "out there".

Alice recoiled, "But what we would be saying or intimating is not true."

Ben replied, "It's not entirely untrue."

"But it's a lie."

Alice was shaken. In her years of student government and social activism lying and half truths had never been a part of it. Her involvement with #YesAllWomen had been liberating. Being a student leader who had introduced and spearheaded it on campus was a seminal event. It was the catalyst for her entering into politics – the greater good.

"I don't think I can do this - and I don't think we should do it." The illusion of a "dream come true" was turning nightmarish.

Ben replied, "The polling puts this race too close to call. If we don't win think about the consequences. What do you think is going to happen if we aren't in office?"

Alice thought about that – their opponent was way over a value line that was etched in granite in her mind. But lying, telling a half truth, not completing a sentence that would change its whole meaning, it was nothing she had ever done before.

Ben interrupted her thinking, "You have to tell me right now if you're not going to do this. Look Alice, you are going to move with us from the campaign into government. Don't mess this up. Are you onboard or not?"

All kinds of thoughts began flashing through Alice's mind like a nightclub strobe light. "It's morally wrong." "This is politics – lying is an accepted practice." "It's unethical – but think about the greater good." "What about my career?" "What about me - will doing this define me?" "Implied isn't lying is it?" "Spin is a grammatical task – it isn't lying."

As in a dream, she heard herself suddenly saying, "Okay." In a daze (that was easy in her sleep deprived state) she set about the task. She kept hearing Lady Gaga speaking in the background "I'm telling you a lie in a vicious effort that you will repeat my lie over and over until it becomes true." Alice kept shaking that out of her head, but it kept coming back. "Oh well."

The election was won by the slimmest of margins. Ben confided to her that based on exit polls the social media campaign she had orchestrated had made a difference, and her work would not be forgotten. It wasn't long before Alice got an appointment to a government agency as an administrative assistant to the Director. Sweet! Doing right for the greater good! The dream was back.

Several months into her job the Director pulled her aside. Alice felt a rush of something. Whatever it was it sure felt good. The Director said, "I talked with Ben at lunch. He told me you were a go-to person that can be trusted."

"*Okay,*" Alice thought with a twinge of excitement.

"I want you to contact these people in the field and I want you to direct them to . . . STOP! I don't want you taking notes!"

"*Really?*" she thought as she felt the excitement begin to drain away.

"Now listen carefully" and the Director spelled out what was wanted, adding "No emails, hard copies, voicemail, no records – do you understand?" The hair on the back of Alice's neck started to tingle. This just didn't seem right. Questioning the Director crossed her mind but she quickly dismissed the thought.

"Let me know immediately when you get this done."

Alice quickly finished the task, and walked into the Director's office and informed her, "Mission accomplished!"

The Director said "Look Alice. When I gave you this task, I could read a bit of hesitancy in your body language."

"You think!" Alice thought.

The Director went on, "This is the way the system works. It doesn't matter who sits in this seat. Imagine the alternative. We are doing the right things for the right reasons. Now, did you leave any paper or electronic trail?"

"No" Alice said.

"Perfect" replied the Director.

It didn't seem perfect, but Alice felt the afterglow of the recognition, and that was good enough. The rest of the day went pretty well although the conversation with the Director never fully went away.

That evening while she was cooking dinner, her Mom called. "How is work going?"

"It's challenging," not untrue thought Alice.

"They are reporting some nasty stuff going on. You're not involved in any of that are you?" her mom asked. What's with moms and their sixth sense?

"Not with anything specific I've seen in the press" Alice replied.

"They just reported on the news that Ben guy who ran the campaign has been called in to testify in front of an oversight committee. Do you still stay in touch with him? He seemed like such a nice man."

"We haven't talked in a long while Mom," Alice replied.

The conversation shifted to usual mother-daughter stuff. Alice's Dad got on the phone before she hung up and told her how proud he was of her.

As soon as Alice hung up she began to cry – "What have I done." After a bit, she took a breath and thought to herself, "I'm doing this for the right reasons. Nobody said it would be easy. It's just the way it is." The sun came up in the morning, and Alice began another day, albeit her "web" a bit more tangled. On the commute in she remembered Mark Twain's remark, "If you tell the truth, you don't have to remember anything." Her job had just ratcheted up a notch in difficulty and her "playbook" was now more complex.

Some organizations have deeply embedded thinking processes carried on for decades. When you become totally immersed, what once was seemingly wrong is right and what's right is wrong. The political arena has become an example of where things often are upside down.

The ethics of public service are spelled out in laws mostly defined by the exchange of influence for what can be measured with money, which leaves a lot of space in which to maneuver. Using only a self-righteous Utilitarian ethical mindset one can justify about anything if one sets their mind to it. When the ethical tests of Rights, Justice, and Virtue get thrown under the bus what are you left with?

Dilemmas are never going away. Considering each alternative and testing them against a complete ethical framework is a path to resolving dilemmas and getting to decision and action that you don't have to stammer about or spin later on. In the absence of "Stop-Think-Test-Act", regardless of sector – public or private – organizations and companies' thinking processes can slide, one decision at a time, from admirable to despicable with matching actions. Corporate Think / Organizational Think starts and ends with leadership. The end justifying the means is a long slippery slope - once on, it is difficult to get back off.

If You Are What You Eat, Your Company Is What It Thinks

Chapter 15

"THE _____ CLUB"

"Club" is an interesting word. It refers equally to a weapon as well as a sandwich. It is used both in nautical and military jargon. Unless you are at lunch, we usually associate the word with the gathering of people with common characteristics, interests, objectives, and for mutual support. In this context, there is a good side as well as a dark side. It depends on whether the club is one of inclusion or exclusion.

Harry was taken aback. "If you want to get anywhere, you're going to have to join the club." When he walked out of his performance review, it was the only thing he could remember. Harry wasn't a stranger to clubs. He belonged to several – from soccer to astronomy. He knew what clubs were from high school and college. There had been a club for almost every subject, but there were also the informal "fit in" clubs too. He didn't fully get this latter type until he learned about Maslow's Theory in his freshman year Psychology course.

As he was walking back to his desk, Sally passed by and asked if he was going to lunch. Without thinking, he said "sure" and reversed directions. At lunch, Harry was still mulling over his performance review. It was upsetting. He had hit a wall that he didn't even know was there.

Sally interrupted his trance, "What are you thinking about?"

Harry blurted out, "Do you belong to *'the club'*?"

Sally said, "What?"

Harry replied, "You know, 'THE CLUB'."

Sally paused and then replied, "Yes I do."

"Okay, how do I get in?"

"You don't. It's for women professionals only."

Harry was dazed. "What do you do? What's the club for?"

"We discuss workplace issues."

"Like what?"

"We network about things like harassment, diversity, not being taken seriously, to rating members of supervision and management and forwarding those ratings into HR to be cranked into evaluations."

Harry was starting to get it – "the Club." That afternoon, Harry began poking around. He couldn't exactly go back and ask his supervisor about "the club" particularly which club without looking totally stupid. What he did discover over the next weeks and months was that just under the surface was an underlying web of 'clubs' each with their interests and affinities, from the women's to the good old boys.

If You Are What You Eat, Your Company Is What It Thinks

He began to see people differently. He started associating people with Dr. Seuss's book the "Sneetches." He saw some people with "stars upon thars" and others without. As he discovered more and more "clubs," Harry came up with a different symbol for each of the "Clubs." Now, as he walked through the halls or sat in a meeting, he saw everyone wearing their symbol. He began to see less and less of the person, just the club icon.

The obvious clubs were "functional." There were the IT club, the HR Club, the Engineering Club, The Management Club, and the list went on from there with clubs within clubs. Harry came to see work, much differently. Under the surface, it was a tribal third world society. There were "warlords" at the head of each club who directed the ebb and flow. He now saw confrontations not about content and ideas but about winning and losing. And if the club wasn't winning it was losing, and who wants to be a member of a loser.

In the midst of Harry struggling with finding the right "Club," disaster struck. The business was overrun by a competitor's innovation. The Engineering Club and the Sales Club had both blown off this competitor as a lightweight. The business had to switch gears quickly into a survival mode jettisoning weight quickly, weight being people. The Clubs went on high alert. Work started looking more like "Lord of the Flies" on steroids. There was plenty of posturing and trumpeting with the pointing of fingers and the musical chairs blame game.

When the axe came down, it was swift and without mercy. Harry hadn't aligned with a club outside his function, and this made him an easy out. On the day of reckoning, Harry was among the many who were escorted off the premises. It was a sad day.

If You Are What You Eat, Your Company Is What It Thinks

Years later when Harry was recruited for a CEO spot, he reflected how disastrous this inside club culture had been. People weren't paying attention to outside the company. The island of the company was their universe. What shocked him was that the club culture permeated his new company. "Clubs" were taking precedence over the customer and the challenges of the business. He successfully dismantled the self-interest clubs and redirected the energy, but it didn't come easily.

"Clubs" are a part of every company. People have a need to belong, to be a part of something bigger. In larger companies "the company" is just too big to be meaningful. So "clubs" will emerge to fill the need. But when they go over the line and start working at cross purposes with the goals of the company, they become a malady drawing energy away from what matters.

The formation of "clubs" is going to happen. They should be managed and elevated by leadership actions bringing them out of the shadows. They can become a part of "the force", or when not acknowledged and groomed they become destructive circles of exclusion and take control of Corporate Think.

What's your club?

EPILOGUE

There is a proverb attributed to Native Americans, the Chinese, and even Benjamin Franklin. It states:

> "Tell me and I'll forget.
>
> Show me, and I may not remember.
>
> Involve me, and I'll understand."

No matter who said it first, this proverb is the riverbed over which "Corporate Think" flows.

Pronouncements, emails, letters, have a rapid decay time. Their memory retention half-life can probably be stated in terms of hours. Demonstrating what you want to communicate is a step up particularly if it is demonstrated frequently and by all members of management. Involving a person in what you are trying to communicate is a high percentage tactic and not easily forgotten.

The continuous looping of Tell-Show-Involve is leadership's teaching process to set and solidify Corporate Think.

Poder es servir

www.ingramcontent.com/pod-product-compliance
Lightning Source LLC
Chambersburg PA
CBHW071226170526
45165CB00003B/1002